D0860355

ART INSTITUTE OF ATLANTA
LIBRARY

DIRECT MAIL MARKETING
D E S I G N

Rockport Publishers, Rockport, Massachusetts
Distributed by North Light Books, Cincinnati, Ohio

DESIGN AND LAYOUT
Sara Day and Poppy Evans

Printed in China

Copyright © 1994 Rockport Publishers, Inc.,

All rights reserved. No part of this book may be reproduced in any form without written permission of the copyright owners. All images in this book have been reproduced with the knowledge and prior consent of the artists concerned and no responsibility is accepted by producer, publisher or printer for any infringement of copyright or otherwise, arising from the contents of this publication. Every effort has been made to ensure that credits accurately comply with information supplied.

First Published in the United States of America by:
Rockport Publishers, Inc.
146 Granite Street
Rockport, MA 01966
Telephone: 508-546-9590
Fax: 508-546-7141
Telex: 5106019284 ROCKORT PUB

Distributed to the book trade and art trade in the U.S. and Canada by:
North Light, an imprint of
F & W Publications
1507 Dana Avenue
Cincinnati, Ohio 45207
Telephone: (513) 531-2222

Other Distribution by:
Rockport Publishers, Inc.
Rockport, Massachusetts 01966

ISBN 1-56496-080-3

10 9 8 7 6 5 4 3 2

CONTENTS

INTRODUCTION 5

PRODUCTS AND SERVICES 7

FUNDRAISING AND RECRUITING 77

SELF-PROMOTION 91

SPECIALTY 131

INDEX 156

Since we started constructing exceptional projects, there's been a lot of change.

The smallest construction details can make a big difference in the success of a project.

Since 1926, Nason and Cullen has been providing building expertise and renovation services to a wide array of clients. From corporations and research facilities to hospitals and educational institutions, we provide cost competitive construction, on time and of high quality. We achieve this through personal service, attention to detail, and modern construction technology.

No matter how large or small, simple or complex, your project receives an exceptional level of workmanship. When it comes to building excellence, that's Nason and Cullen's bottom line.

That is why Nason and Cullen consistently delivers an exceptional level of quality.

Nason and Cullen, Inc.
Builders and Construction Managers

It's true that a quarter went a lot further back in 1926. One thing that hasn't changed since Nason and Cullen opened its doors is our solid commitment to quality construction. It's the foundation on which every one of our projects is built.

To each client, we bring old-fashioned personal service and attention to detail, combined with modern construction technology. The result is consistently timeless. Regardless of size and complexity, you can count on Nason and Cullen to make your next project a success.

Nason and Cullen is still worth the investment.

Nason and Cullen, Inc.
Builders and Construction Managers
Delaware Corporate Center
Wilmington, Delaware 19803
(302) 477-

Du Pont Merck
Delmarva Power and Light
Rollins
DISCOVER CARD

DELAWARE
Ciba Geigy
Grotto's Pizza
DelleDonne Associates
Brandywine Realty and Dev

HIMONT

University of Delaware
AMERICAS INC.

INTRODUCTION

Direct mail marketing experts say it takes approximately three to five seconds for the average consumer to decide whether to open a piece of mail or pitch it. This probably comes as no surprise to most of us who are accustomed to sifting through a daily stack of seemingly endless mail at our offices, only to come home and find another barrage of mail waiting for us in our mailboxes.

Knowing how hard it is to get most of us to open and read a direct mail promotion, those who conceive and design them will do just about anything to pique our interest. Some will even go so far as to suggest on the outer wrapper that urgent information or fortune lies within. We've all seen mailers that mimic express mail packages or appear as though a check with our name on it is tucked inside.

Direct Mail Marketing ignores such obvious ploys which are rarely effective in eliciting a response in favor of direct mail pieces that are so artfully and cleverly conceived they never fail to be noticed, opened and read. The promotional mailers within these pages achieve their purpose because we respond so positively to the beauty and intelligence of their design.

They are unique in their ability to provoke our curiosity by dazzling or intriguing us. They catch our eye because their color, unusual shape, or size immediately isolates them from ordinary mail. They may display a dramatic image or a statement that piques our interest or catches our attention. A wrapper made of sumptuous material which begs to be touched will beckon the beholder to handle, open and discover what lies within.

An unusual or irresistible outer wrapper will catch our attention, but an effective promotional mailer must follow through by delivering its message clearly and forcefully. We must be compelled to read the promotion and respond to it. Eye-catching graphics or an intriguing headline set in a reader-friendly typeface will prompt us to scan and ultimately absorb the message. The follow-through will be made so easy that there will be no confusion about how to respond to it.

An effective direct mail promotion must also be a well-designed package, compact and modular so that all components fit neatly together. The hierarchy of the information within must be presented in such a way that each component will have a level of visual impact appropriate to its level of importance. Like a kimono, it should reveal many layers of information, a single layer at a time as we open it, leading us through its message in a logical manner. It will also be unfailing in its consistency. Like a visual symphony, all components of a comprehensive mailing will work together to project a unified image in support of the mission of the piece, whether it be to sell a product, elicit support, or initiate business.

Finally, an effective direct mail promotion should be unforgettable. If it fails to generate an immediate response in us, it should at least leave a favorable impression, and possibly a lasting one that will prompt a response at a future date.

It falls upon the graphic designer of a direct mail promotion to accomplish all of this with the image and the tastes of us and the client in mind and, at the same time, meet postal requirements and the postage budget for the piece as well. Accomplishing all of this on time and on budget can be a formidable challenge in itself. Graphic designers can take pride when they acheive these results with a piece that just happens to also be beautifully designed, as well.

- Poppy Evans

Poppy Evans is a graphic designer and author of many books and articles on the graphic arts. She teaches graphic design and computer publishing at the college level.

COLUMBIA HOUSE
1400 North Fruitridge Avenue
Terre Haute, Indiana 47811

Listen to quality.
(Get 8 CDs FREE!)

Excuse me?

I didn't hear that . . .

SAMPLE PACKAGE   AFB/1022003345
JUNE 91 NMA PKG113P
ANYWHERE, CZ 00599-9999

Columbia music House club
Get 8 CDs FREE
(with membership)

Listen to this.
Join Columbia House   Get 8 CDs FREE
(with membership)

Listen to these sounds.

This is it. The perfect way to acquire the CD collection you've always wanted. And it's so simple. From the extensive selection of CDs listed in this booklet, choose 8 and we'll send them to you FREE! After that all you have to is buy 6 more CDs at regular Club prices in the coming three years. So don't miss out on this great opportunity. Pick your favorites and join today!

Pick 8 FREE
(with membership)

†Selections with two numbers are 2-CD sets and count as two selections— write each number in a separate box.

You heard right. Columbia House is giving away FREE music! Yes, 8 CDs FREE when you join now. Sounds good? Wait'll you hear this. You can choose your 8 CDs from a huge and current list of all your favorite artists. How does the pulsating rhythm of Gloria Estefan sound to you? The soulful melodies of Billy Joel? Maybe you're into R&B artists like Anita Baker or Quincy Jones. How 'bout Rap? We've got the latest and greatest from the best of today's rappers.

Okay, so if that doesn't sound right up your alley, listen to this . . . we've got an impressive collection of classical CDs too. Like Horowitz, Stern and Yo-Yo Ma. Every jazz great from Sonny Rollins to George Benson to Chick Corea. Country stars like Randy Travis and Garth Brooks. Come on now, some of this must be perking up your ears. Maybe you go for classic rock, The Doors? The Stones? Led Zepplin? Maybe Hard Rock? Easy Listening? We've got it all. Whatever your musical tastes, we've got plenty to choose from. In fact, Columbia House has over 2500

Join now and get 8 CDs FREE! Then, over the next 3 years, buy at least 6 more at our regular Club prices. All in all, that's 14 CDs at an average price of just $8.30 each! (Includes shipping and handling.)

Columbia House has over 2500 great selections to choose from. The

3 MORE WAYS TO SAVE
Here's something else you'll want to hear about!

1 SPECIAL BONUSES
When you join Columbia House and order your first CD selection now, you pay just $6.95. That's 50% or more off our regular Club prices. Not only does that save you money, but you'll also get a bonus CD FREE! All in all, that's 10 CDs for less than the price of one.

2 PREFERRED MEMBER PURCHASE PLAN
As soon as you've completed your enrollment agreement, for every CD you buy at regular Club prices, you get another CD at half price.

3 SUPER SALES
When you become a member, you'll regularly receive a Columbia House magazine filled with hundreds of selections, many on sale! CDs for as little as $7.99! Plus special "Members Only" offers on T-shirts and posters!

PRODUCTS AND SERVICES

1 This Twin Valley Popcorn promotional package is sent to consumers and retailers. It includes a postcard, general info folder, and catalog sheet with an order form.

Design Firm: Love Packaging Group
Art Director/Designer: Tracy Holdeman
Illustrator: Tracy Holdeman
Client: Twin Valley Popcorn

2 "This is not a foreign language," states this mailer for an auto repair shop which wanted to promote the addition of Asian makes to its list of cars serviced. "The client resisted the tendency to include a lot of copy," notes Sayles. "It's short, to the point, and it worked."

Design Firm: Sayles Graphic Design
Art Director/Designer: John Sayles
Illustrator: John Sayles
Client: Beckley Imports

3 A newly formed digital type foundry, established by designer Carlos Segura, promoted its fonts by sending off a variety of promotional items in an intriguing drawstring bag. "This promotion literally put us on the map," says Segura.

Design Firm: Segura, Inc.
Art Director/Designer: Carlos Segura
Client: T-26

1

2

3

1 This series of postcards was used to help generate advertising for a new trade magazine. "We had to position *Ray Gun* as an 'on the edge' magazine yet communicate a message to potential advertisers," says principal Eric Boelts. "This piece reflects both concerns."

Design Firm: Boelts Brothers Design, Inc.
Art Director: Jackson Boelts, Eric Boelts
Designer/Illustrator: Jackson Boelts,
Eric Boelts, Kerry Stratford
Client: Ray Gun Magazine

2 Sent to targeted advertisers for a special section within *AOPA Pilot* magazine, this piece promotes the low cost of advertising in this issue. "Besides being a good vehicle for our client's message, the recipient had a good time with the promo," relates Eric Boelts.

Design Firm: Boelts Bros. Design, Inc.
Art Director/Designer: Jackson Boelts, Eric Boelts
Contributors: Michelle Ramiriz, Denis Beran,
Gary Benzel
Client: AOPA Pilot magazine

3 This telecommunications firm promoted its service advantages to small businesses with this series of promotional brochures. The brochures caught the attention of national media, bringing additional exposure to the client.

Design Firm: Vaughn Wedeen Creative
Art Director/Designer: Steve Wedeen
Photographer: Michael Barley
Illustrator: Kevin Tolman
Client: US West Communications

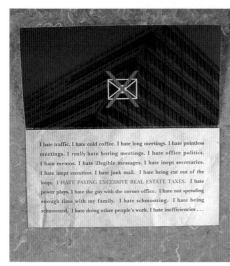 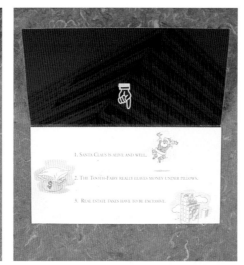 

 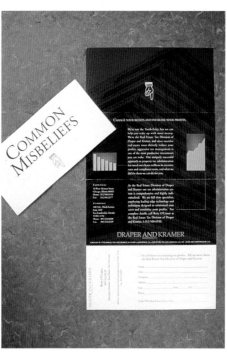 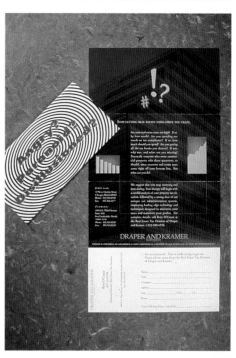

1 This unique approach to promoting real estate investments generated a great response. "We received enormously positive feedback from our client," says firm principal, Patricia Bukur.

Design Firm: Bukur Design Group
Art Director: Patricia Bukur
Designer: Patricia Bukur, Michael Romane
Illustrator: Ken Simpson
Client: Draper & Kramer

2

3

2 Art and photography are effectively merged in this fashion mailer for men's contemporary clothing. The piece was sent to customers on a select mailing list to reach fashion-conscious consumers that were not as easily reached through traditional media.

Design Firm: Dayton's, Hudson's, Marshall Field
Art Director/Designer: Cheryl Watson
Illustrator: Anthony Russo
Clients: Dayton's, Hudson's, Marshall Field

3 This direct mail promotion was sent to promote a special section of *AOPA Pilot* magazine that pushed high-end, turbine aviation products. "It got the recipient involved with the piece while communicating the client's message," says principal Eric Boelts.

Design Firm: Boelts Brothers Design, Inc.
Art Director: Jackson Boelts, Eric Boelts
Designer: Jackson Boelts, Eric Boelts, Todd Fedell
Client: AOPA Pilot magazine

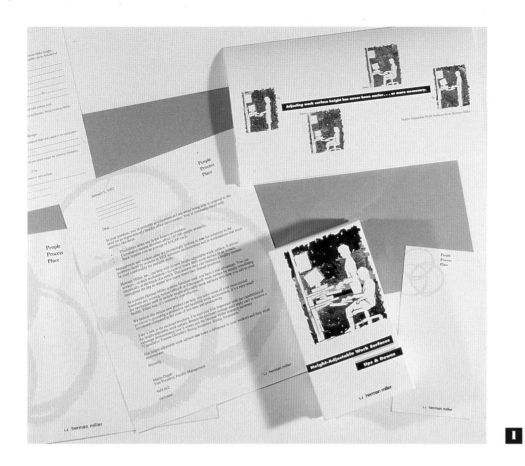

1

2

1 This multicomponent mailer was used to generate leads for Herman Miller's sales force.

Design Firm: Jane Ross & Associates
Photographer: HMI Stock
Client: Herman Miller, Inc.

2 This box mailer attracts attention with graphics that wrap around the sides. Inside, a die-cut brochure features "pop-out" photos.

Design Firm: Sayles Graphic Design
Art Director/Designer: John Sayles
Illustrator: John Sayles
Client: Crowley-Mandelbaum Commercial Real Estate Brokers

3

3 This paper promotion succeeded in attracting attention and stimulating controversy by effectively integrating art and photography with political subject matter. "Interest was generated in areas I wouldn't have expected," notes designer Craig Berhnardt who says Gilbert Paper heard from many nondesigners.

Design Firm: Bernhardt Fudyma Design Group
Art Director: Craig Bernhardt
Designer: Iris Brown
Client: Gilbert Paper Company

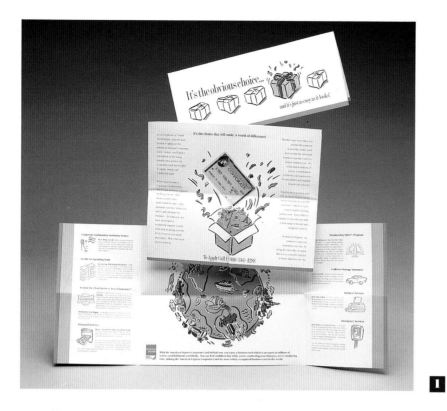

1 American Express commissioned this promotion to send to approximately 35,000 employees of a single corporation. It was successful in convincing them to choose American Express for their business sravel.

Design Firm: Mike Quon Design Office
Art Director: Mike Quon, H. Samkange
Designer: Mike Quon
Illustrator: Mike Quon
Client: American Express Company

2 Layers of information tucked neatly inside an intriguing black box succeeded in showcasing a unique product line with sophistication and flair.

Design Firm: O&J Design, Inc.
Art Director: Andrzej J. Olejniczak
Designer: Andrzej J. Olejniczak,
I. Clara Kim
Photographer: Scott Bowron
Client: Peipers & Kojen

3 (Opposite page) Intriguing numbers suggesting a business solution lie within this business-to-business mailer. Designer Mike Quon says New York Telephone wanted to stress business relationships and accessibility with this piece.

Design Firm: Mike Quon Design Office
Art Directors: Mike Quon, T. Alpert
Designer: Mike Quon
Illustrator: Mike Quon
Client: New York Telephone

The Customer Partnership Program matches senior executives

One

from the region's premier companies with executives from

On

New York Telephone, one on one. This forum allows decision

One

makers to understand both sides of the business equation.

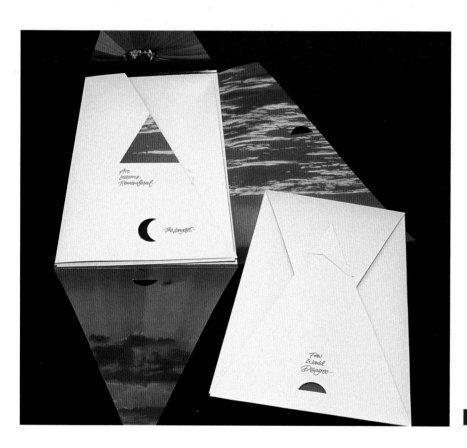

1 Introducing retailers to this new brand of salsa required combining attractive packaging with an engaging brochure. Designer Hector Garcia says the piece generated so many inquiries, "the client went through about 10,000 of their follow-up fliers in just three months."

Design Firm: Mac By Night Design
Art Director/Designer: Damion Hickman, Hector Garcia
Photographer: Scott Montgomery
Illustrator: Damion Hickman
Client: Napa Valley Gourmet Salsa

2 Always An Adventure is a company that makes learning fun. Its promotional mailer draws attention with its odd shape and surprise within each fold. Principal Ivan Angelic says his client was really pleased with the feedback the mailer generated and at one point was introduced as "the people with the great folder."

Design Firm: Hoffmann & Angelic Design
Art Director: Andrea Hoffman
Designer: Ivan Angelic
Photographer: David Allen
Calligrapher: Ivan Angelic
Client: Always An Adventure

3 The primary objective of this promotion was to increase overall product awareness among produce buyers and communicate that the product is sweet, not hot.

Design Firm: BaileySpiker, inc
Art Director: Paul Spiker
Designer: Dave Fiedler, Steve Perry
Photographer: Rudy Muller
Illustrator: Steve Perry
Client: FreshWorld Farms

1

1 "Strong Points" defines the mission and guiding principles of this serious-minded promotion for a reinsurance company.

Design Firm: WYD Design, Inc.
Art Director: David Dunkelberger, Frank J. Oswald
Designer: Scott Kuykendall, David Dunkelberger
Photographer: Schaffer/Smith
Client: Zurich Reinsurance Centre, Inc.

2 Tips for small businesses is the "soft sell" used to pitch this telecommunications firm. The brochure has staying power as a valuable resource for the small businesses that received it.

Design Firm: Vaughn Wedeen Creative
Art Director/Designer: Steve Wedeen
Photographer: Michael Barley
Client: US West Communications

2

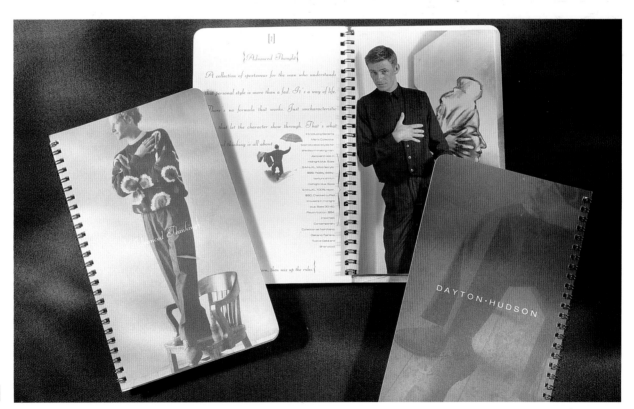

1 "When designers are your audience, you need to do a creative mail piece, even on a limited budget," says John Sayles in describing this mailer. This self-mailer opens to reveal a poster.

Design Firm: Sayles Graphic Design
Art Director: John Sayles
Designer: John Sayles
Illustrator: John Sayles
Client: James River Paper

2 This fashion mailer promoting men's contemporary clothing conveys a look of casual elegance well suited to the upscale image the client wanted to project.

Design Firm: Dayton's, Hudson's, Marshall Field
Art Director/Designer: Cheryl Watson
Photographer: Bob Frame
Client: Dayton's, Hudson's

1

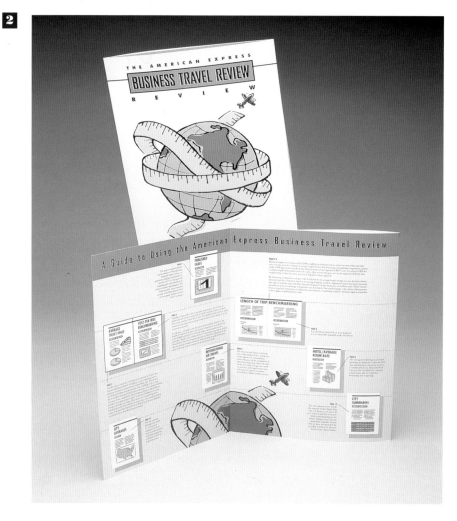

2

1 This upscale furniture company sent out a packet of four-page brochures with related collateral.

Design Firm: Vaughn Wedeen Creative
Art Director/Designer: Rick Vaughn
Photographer: Robert Reck
Client: Taos Furniture

2 American Express commissioned this business travel guide for travel agents to send to prospective card users.

Design Firm: Mike Quon Design Office
Art Director: Mike Quon, J. Schofield
Designer: Mike Quon
Illustrator: Mike Quon
Client: American Express Company

3 (Opposite page) To differentiate Active Graphics, a four-color printer, from its competition designer Mark Oldach played up the firm's name with colorful photos of active wear. "Their name recognition has increased substantially since then," says Oldach.

Design Firm: Mark Oldach Design
Art Director: Mark Oldach
Designer: Don Emery
Photographer: Gregory Gaymont
Client: Active Graphics

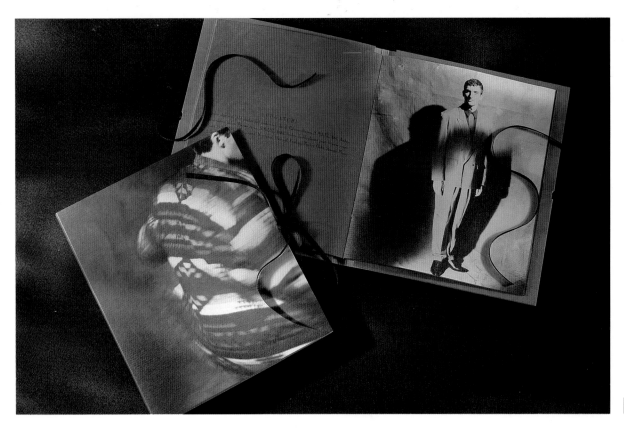

1 An elegant invitation to an art glass exhibit was conceived to draw customers and convey a sophisticated image. The heavy card, featuring two of the pieces from the traveling exhibit, was wrapped in handmade paper.

Design Firm: Dayton's
Art Director/Designer: Cheryl Watson
Photographer: Charles Purvis
Client: Dayton's

2 This fashion mailer promotes men's contemporary clothing. Says designer Cheryl Watson, "Its objective was to create a memorable piece that the customer would respond to and keep longer than the average direct mail piece."

Design Firm: Dayton's, Hudson's, Marshall Field
Art Director/Designer: Cheryl Watson
Photographer: José Picayo
Client: Dayton's, Hudson's

1 Conceived as an "image piece" for the retail outlets involved, this fashion mailer's humble cover is at once intriguing yet elegantly understated.

Design Firm: Dayton's, Hudson's, Marshall Field
Art Director/Designer: Cheryl Watson
Photographer: Bob Frame
Client: Dayton's, Hudson's

2 An invitation to a fashion event uses custom lettering to convey a regal look and promote an upscale image. "It had to communicate, at a glance, the cause, variety of entertainment, and exquisite setting," says designer Cheryl Watson.

Design Firm: Dayton's, Hudson's, Marshall Field
Art Director: Cheryl Watson
Designer: Cheryl Watson, Margo Chase
Photographer: James
Client: Hudson's

1

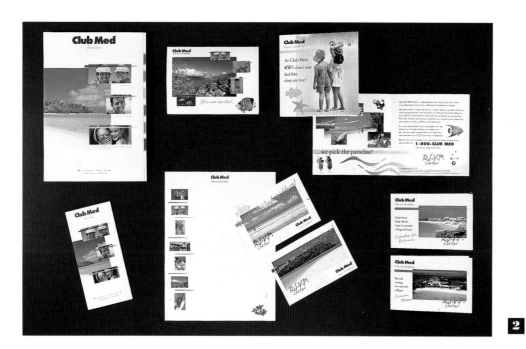

2

1 This series of off-size postcards aggressively positioned First Impression, a one-to-three-color printer, as a cost-effective alternative to larger printers. Mailed quarterl, over a three-year period, "Their business tripled," says Oldach.

Design Firm: Mark Oldach Design
Art Director: Mark Oldach
Designers: Mark Oldach, Mark Meyer
Client: First Impression

2 This multicomponent promotional packet is mailed to prospective members of Club Med. "The format is cheap to mail and still very efficient in pulling bookings," says Laurent Hubert of Club Med. One of the mailings, costing $9,500, rang up sales in excess of $250,000.

Design Firm: O & J Design, Inc.
Art Director/Designer: Andrew Jablonski
Client: Club Med, Inc.

1

1 This colorful piece, which went out to over 100,000 New York City–based businesses, promotes special events at New York City's World Trade Center.

Design Firm: Mike Quon Design Office
Art Director/Designer: Mike Quon
Illustrator: Mike Quon
Client: World Trade Center

2 This series of four self-mailers promoting employee benefits generated a terrific response. "It renewed my faith in direct mail marketing," says client Bill Wackerman, Marketing Manager at *Business Week*.

Design Firm: Parham Santana, Inc.
Art Director: John Parham
Designer: Katherine Inglis
Illustrator: John Labbé
Client: Business Week magazine

2

1

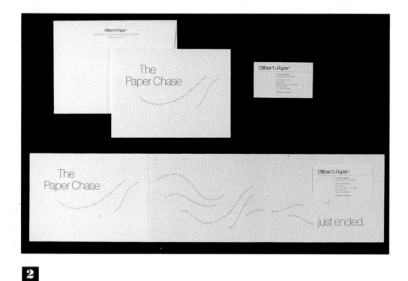

2

3

1 A simple duotone is used to suggest the removal of dirt (the black screen) from a rug-like texture used to spell "dirty class."

Design Firm: Gunnar Swanson Design Office
Art Director/Designer: Gunnar Swanson
Photographer: Anthony Nex
Client: Mark the Carpetbagger

2 This promotional mailer for Gilbert Paper announces the arrival of a new specifica-tion representative in Manhattan. "Gilbert's new rep received a lot of calls as a result of this piece," says designer Susan Chait.

Design Firm: Lebowitz/Gould/Design, Inc.
Art Director/Designer: Susan Chait
Copywriter: Ron Brothers
Client: Gilbert Paper

3 "Look into your future" states this promotional mailer for US West. The crystal ball and brochure were sent to employees who achieved performance goals.

Design Firm: Vaughn Wedeen Creative
Art Director/Designer: Steve Wedeen
Illustrator: Steve Wedeen, Chip Wyley
Client: US West Communications

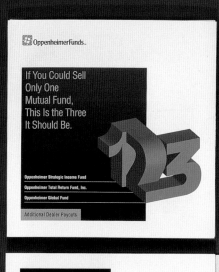

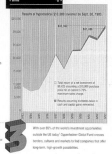

1 Numbers with impact get a solid, three-dimensional treatment. "The emphasis on prime numbers and the relationship to their payouts attracted brokers' attention," says client Julia O'Neal of Oppenheimer.

Design Firm: O&J Design, Inc.
Art Director/Designer: Andrzej J. Olejniczak
Client: Oppenheimer Management

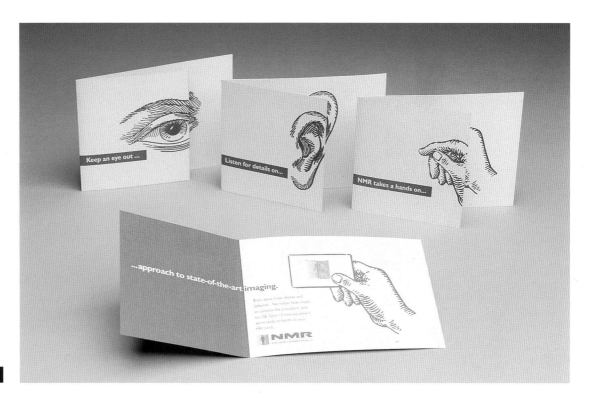

2

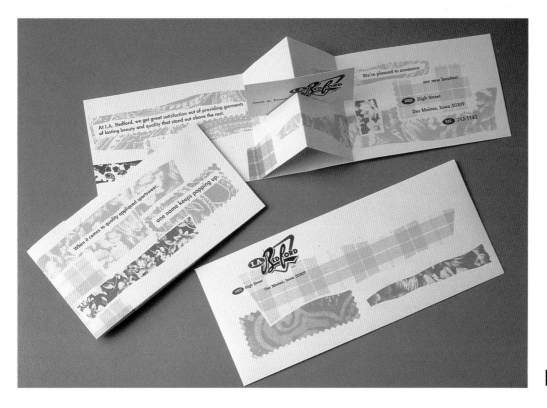

3

1 (Opposite page) This mailer, promoting a new hair-care product to salon owners, does double duty as a point-of-purchase display.

Design Firm: Mike Quon Design Office
Art Director: Mike Quon, Scott Fishoff
Designer: Mike Quon
Photographer: Jack Reznicki
Illustrator: Mike Quon
Client: Clairol

2 "Keep an eye out..." is one of a number of teaser lines depicted on this series of promotional postcards.

Design Firm: Mike Quon Design Office
Art Director: Mike Quon, J. Rosenberg
Illustrator: Mike Quon
Client: NMR

3 "One name keeps popping up." This statement is literally portrayed in the unique "pop-up" feature of this promotional mailer.

Design Firm: Sayles Graphic Design
Art Director/Designer: John Sayles
Illustrator: John Sayles
Client: I.A. Bedford

1

2

1 The first mailing in this series carries the slogan, "Here's an outlet for you." The package contents—an electrical outlet— reinforces the appliance theme.

Design Firm: Sayles Graphic Design
Art Director/Designer: John Sayles
Illustrator: John Sayles
Client: Maytag Company

2 A follow-up mailer ties into the theme with its message and a bonus—its message lights up! "This two-part mailing generated a lot of attention," says Sayles. "Let's face it, when you get something in the mail that actually lights up, people notice!"

Design Firm: Sayles Graphic Design
Art Director/Designer: John Sayles
Illustrator: John Sayles
Client: Maytag Company

1

2

1 Generating leads for a new furniture product required a promotional mailer that captured the recipient's attention and, at the same time, conveyed information about the new product line.

Design Firm: Herman Miller
Art Director/Designer: Yang Kim
Illustrator: Yang Kim
Photographer: Nick Merrick, Hedrich Blessing
Client: Herman Miller

2 This direct mail piece promotes a new, Japanese-owned television studio in New York City. There was no studio at the time the promotion was being conceived and produced. "All we had to work from were architectural renderings," says its designer Mike Quon.

Design Firm: Mike Quon Design Office
Art Director/Designer: Mike Quon
Illustrator: Mike Quon
Client: NTV International Corporation

1 This series of six postcards was sent out at weekly intervals to encourage targeted recipients to advertise in *Aviation UA*. The "North, South, East, West" theme reinforced the magazine's broad audience. "They (the postcards) made quite an impact," says designer Eric Boelts.

Design Firm: Boelts Bros. Design, Inc.
Art Director: Jackson Boelts, Eric Boelts
Designer: Jackson Boelts, Eric Boelts
Illustrator: Jackson Boelts
Client: AOPA's *Aviation USA* magazine

2 Mailed to printers, this brochure promotes a recyled line of paper with the tagline, "O What A ReLeaf."

Design Firm: Sayles Graphic Design
Art Director/Designer: John Sayles
Illustrator: John Sayles
Client: Howard Paper

This is a book about Jack.

Jack can't read.

Jack's favorite niece has a brand new book. She wants him to read it to her. He wishes he could.

1

Jack goes to lunch. He can't read the menu so he orders the special. Jack's in for a surprise.

1 This paper promotion, entitled "Jack Can't Read," was designed to push the press capabilities of Gilbert Oxford as well as express concern for illiteracy. "It works as a promotion, grabbing the design audience with color and graphics," says Wedeen, adding, "It's also been well received by literacy groups."

Design Firm: Vaughn Wedeen Creative
Art Director/Designer: Steve Wedeen, Rick Vaughn, Gary Cascio
Illustrator: Gary Cascio
Client: Gilbert Paper

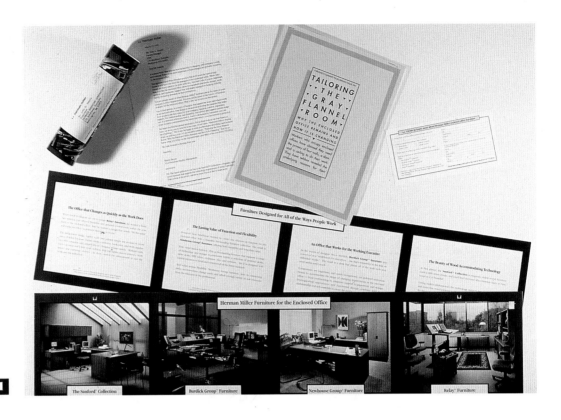

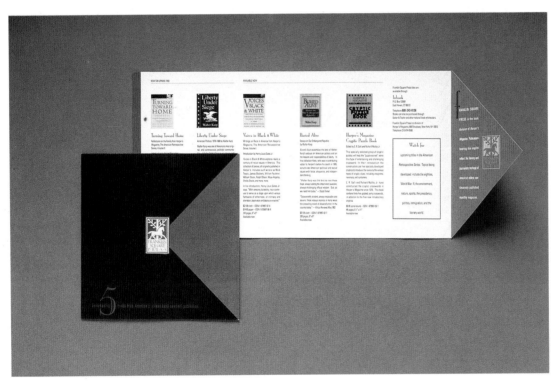

1 Packaged in a tube to set it apart from other mail, this combination of items was used to generate leads for a follow-up call by Herman Miller's sales team.

Design Firm: Holland Mark Martin
Art Director/Designer: Bill Briggs
Client: Herman Miller, Inc.

2 This sophisticated self-mailer succeeded in catching the attention of Harper's upscale readership. According to designer Victoria Peslak, it sold a record-breaking number of books.

Design Firm: Platinum Design, Inc.
Art Director: Victoria Peslak
Designer: Ava Schlesinger
Copywriter: Ava Schlesinger
Client: Harper's magazine

1

2

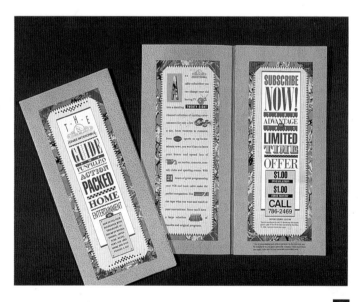

3

1 After designing a logo for Hillside Neighborhood, designer John Sayles fashioned a pen set which was sent as part of a promotional mailing to attract developers to the site.

Design Firm: Sayles Graphic Design
Art Director/Designer: John Sayles
Illustrator: John Sayles
Client: Hillside Neighborhood

2 This slegant catalog sells hard by presenting fine art with a playful edge. According to its designer, Andrzej Olejniczak, "It commands attention, communicates with clarity and, most of all, rewards the reader for time well spent with it."

Design Firm: O&J Design, Inc.
Art Director: Andrzej J. Olejniczak
Designer: Andrzej J. Olejniczak, I. Clara Kim
Illustrator: Seymour Chwast
Client: Sotheby's

3 Bright colors and a charming mix of graphic elements give this cable company's promotional mailer a cozy, informal look.

Design Firm: Vaughn Wedeen Creative
Art Director: Steve Weeden
Designer: Steve Weeden, Daniel Michael Flynn
Illustrator: Daniel Michael Flynn, Kevin Tolman, Lendy McCullough
Client: Jones Intercable

1 This promotional folder is mailed to prospective patients to promote a physical rehabilitation center. Each insert tells the story of a former patient's recovery. "The center was pleased with the caring yet professional image it projects," says David Marks, creative director for Muller & Company.

Design Firm: Muller & Company
Art Director/Designer: John Muller
Photographer: Tal Wilson, Mike Regnier
Client: Saint Francis Medical Center

2 This mail order catalog for a coffee company represents a new brand identity that Hornall Anderson developed for this client. "They felt like we had secured the soul of their business," says firm principal Jack Anderson in describing his client's enthusiastic acceptance of the new look.

Design Firm: Hornall Anderson Design Works
Art Director: Jack Anderson
Designer: Jack Anderson, Julie Tanagi-Lock, Julie Keenan, Lian Ng
Photographer: Darrell Peterson
Illustrator: Julia LaPine
Client: Starbucks Coffee Company

3 (Opposite page) "Listen to This" is the tagline that unifies the various parts of this multicomponent mailing. "This piece was the client's first break from the traditional white envelope," says firm principal Clare Ultimo. "We recommended they use an envelope with a see-through window. Everyone was really intrigued by it."

Design Firm: Ultimo Inc.
Art Director: Clare Ultimo
Designer: Christine Cortina
Illustrator: Emma Crawford
Client: Columbia House

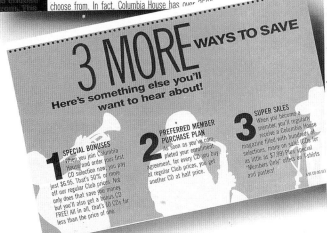

1

1 Focusing on the letter "H" as its theme, this brochure promoted a paper line with a name that begins with the same letter.

Design Firm: Little & Company
Art Director: Paul Wharton
Designer: Ted Riley
Copywriter: Sandra Bucholtz
Client: Cross Pointe Paper Corp.

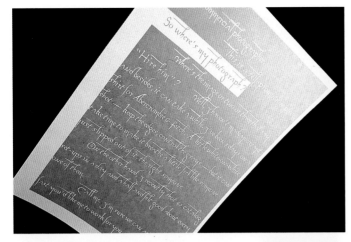

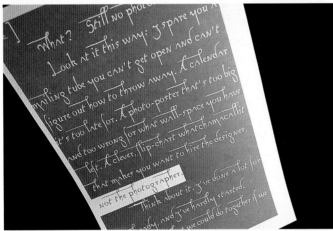

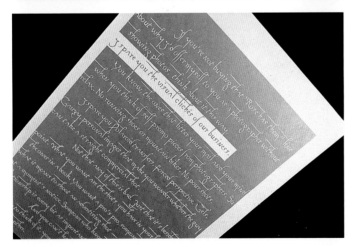

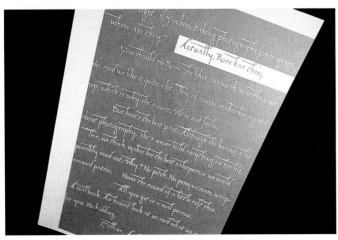

2

1

1 An introductory campaign, consisting of twelve elegantly rendered letters, helped to put this newly established photography studio on the map. Each is a sincere request for business—disarming in its frankness. "The campaign was a definite success," says firm principal Catherine Schmeltz. "It opened lots of doors for this photographer."

Design Firm: Schmeltz & Warren
Art Director/Designer: Crit Warren
Client: John Strange & Associates

2 A custom-designed container houses the "guts" of this self-mailer's message: a computer disk with an interactive lesson on how to make money in the stock market. The mailing's sophisticated audience responded positively to this high-tech approach.

Design Firm: Supon Design Group, Inc.
Creative Director: Supon Phornirunlit
Art Director: Andrew Dolan
Designer: Apisak Saibua
Client: The NASDAQ Stock Market

1

1 Showing off the printing capabilities of text with a laid finish meant pushing the limits of the stock. "This piece extended traditional perceptions of how a laid finish stock performs," says Little & Company art director Mike Lizama.

Design Firm: Little & Company
Art Director/Designer: Mike Lizama
Client: Cross Pointe Paper Corp.

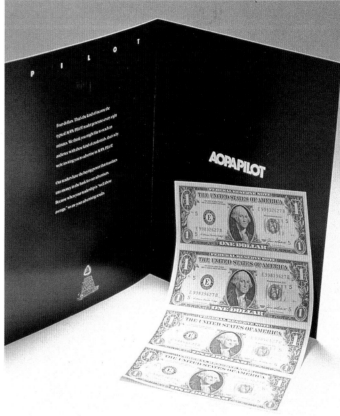

1 These promotional mailings were sent to advertisers as a thank-you gift for their business. The scheme went over so well, six different mailings were conceived and designed by Boelts Bros. to be mailed out every two months over a period of a year.

Design Firm: Boelts Bros. Design, Inc.
Art Director: Jackson Boelts, Eric Boelts
Designer: Jackson Boelts, Eric Boelts, Kerry Stratford
Illustrator: Bob Case
Client: AOPA Pilot

2 Boelts Bros. enclosed four uncut dollar bills to emphasize this mailer's theme. This unusual piece prompted a huge response. "Many of our client's advertisers called them to find out if the money was actually real," relates firm principal Jackson Boelts.

Design Firm: Boelts Bros. Design, Inc.
Art Director: Jackson Boelts, Eric Boelts
Designer: Jackson Boelts, Eric Boelts, Kerry Stratford
Illustrator: Bob Case
Contributors: Denis Beran, Michelle Ramirez
Client: AOPA Pilot

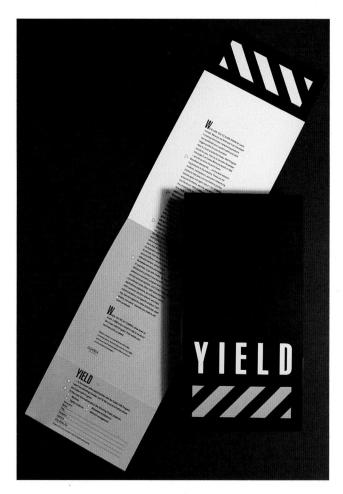

1 The outside of this eye-catching self-mailer sets the theme for copy within suggesting that the reader slow down and consider the benefits of the product it promotes. Codex was pleased with the 5 percent response rate the piece "yielded."

Design Firm: The Brownstone Group
Art Director/Designer: Marc English
Client: Codex

2 Promoting a software upgrade to busy executives and computer experts required spelling out benefits in a direct and concise manner. "This was Meta's first attempt at direct mail marketing," says designer Marc English. "With the help of this mailing, they achieved their sales goal."

Designer: Marc English: Design
Art Director/Designer: Marc English
Client: Meta Software Corp.

3 (Opposite page) The printers, print buyers and designers who received this corrugated box had a hard time resisting the urge to open it. The kit was designed to inform, excite and persuade its audience to specify the line of papers it promoted.

Design Firm: Grafik Communications, Ltd.
Creative Team: Melanie Bass, Gregg Glaviano, Judy F. Kirpich
Copywriter: Jake Pollard
Photographer: Claude Vasquez
Client: Gilbert Papers

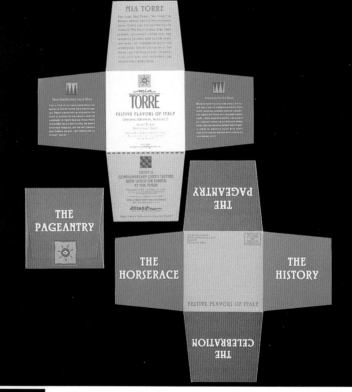

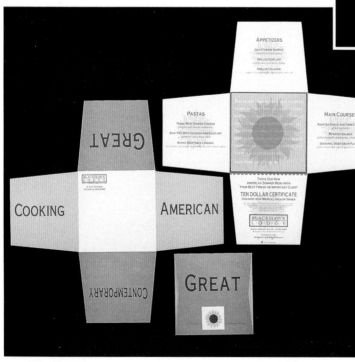

❙ These cleverly folded self-mailers did their job, substantially increasing business at the two restaurants they promoted. Mailings in quantities ranging from 12,000 to 35,000 yielded responses ranging from 10 to 25 percent.

Design Firm: The Levy Restaurants
Creative Director/Designer: Marcy Lansing
Illustrator: Marcy Lansing
Client: Blackhawk Lodge/Mia Torre

1

1 This paper promotion, mailed to CEOs and
communication executives at Fortune 1000
companies, explains how the paper mill can
recycle office waste into new, recycled paper.
"The response to this piece has been terrific,"
says Little & Company principal Paul Wharton.
"I believe that Cross Pointe has quadrupled their
sales for this program."

Design Firm: Little & Company
Art Director: Paul Wharton
Designer: Garin Ipsen
Illustrator: Guy Billout
Client: Cross Pointe Paper Corp.

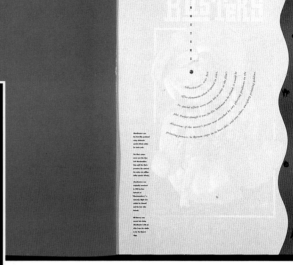

1 Showing off a printer's capabilities provided an opportunity for showcasing great design. This promotional brochure and series of posters opened doors for the client, and Rickabaugh Graphics. "It's cinched a lot of deals for us," says firm principal Eric Rickabaugh.

Design Firm: Rickabaugh Graphics
Art Director/Designer: Eric Rickabaugh
Photographer: Paul Poplis
Illustrator: Fred Warter Michael Tennyson Smith, Eric Rickabaugh
Client: Byrum Lithographing

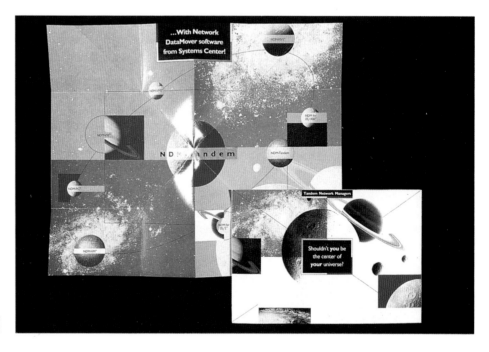

1 This promotional mailing consisted of a brochure and a series of notecards boxed in custom casing. "The client wanted to sell college professors on their textbook," says firm principal Clare Ultimo, who came up with the idea of printing the book's art plates on notecards. "The idea was very successful," she says. "Everybody wanted them."

Design Firm: Ultimo Inc.
Art Director: Clare Ultimo
Designer: Joanne Obarowski, Clare Ultimo
Client: Macmillan Publishing Co.

2 Interplanetary visuals from stock photography provided a budget-conscious theme for this product promotion. According to the piece's design team, the mailer's clever folding and intriguing imagery worked, generating a 5 percent reply rate in an market area where 2 percent is the norm.

Design Firm: Grafik Communications, Ltd.
Design Team Members: Ned Drew, Judy F. Kirpich
Illustrator: Ned Drew
Client: Systems Center, Inc.

3 (Opposite page) Targeted to television advertisers and affiliates, this package consisted of a folder, custom letterhead, demo tape, and brochure. The client wanted to correct an erroneous impression that its programming was ethnically focused. "They wanted to project a more diverse image," says its creative director, Supon Phornirunlit. " This piece accomplished that."

Design Firm: Supon Design Group, Inc.
Creative Director: Supon Phornirunlit
Art Director: Andrew Dolan
Designer: Andrew Berman
Client: Black Entertainment Television

1

1 This combination poster/paper specifier does double duty as an effective paper promotion and a useful reference chart.

Design Firm: Grafik Communications, Ltd.
Art Director: Judy F. Kirpich
Designer: Julie Sebastianelli, Lynn Umemoto
Illustrator: Henrik Drescher
Calligraphy: Henrik Drescher, Melanie Bass
Client: Frank Parsons Paper Company, Inc.

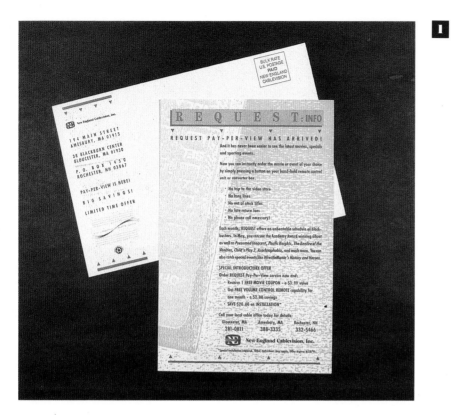

1 This promotional mailer needed to educate television viewers on how easy it is to order pay-for-view movies. A discount incentive also helped to lure customers, resulting in a sales increase of 75% in that segment of the client's business.

Design Firm: Lewis Design
Art Director/Designer: Thom Lewis
Photographer: Thom Lewis
Client: New England Cablevision

2 Promoting a newly formed accounting systems consulting firm required a brochure that was first of all affordable. The client also wanted to project an image that was fresh, yet business-like. "They're a young company," says designer Lynn St. Pierre. "They felt the design of this brochure was exactly what they were looking for."

Design Firm: Lynn St. Pierre Graphic Design
Art Director/Designer: Lynn St. Pierre
Copywriter: Toni Yoss
Illustrator: Kyle Raetz
Client: FRC Consulting, Inc.

1

2

1 This brochure promised a chance to participate in a drawing for a free trip to those who visited a trade show booth. Mailed two weeks before the event, it succeeded in luring traffic to the client's booth. Ten percent of those who received the mailing showed up to enter their name in the drawing.

Design Firm: The Brownstone Group
Art Director/Designer: Marc English
Illustrator: Marc English
Client: Codex

2 Screenprinted on chipboard, this hand-bound brochure arrived in a jute twine-wrapped box. It's unusual "outback" look caught the attention of its audience. This unusual package also caught the attention of the design community and was the focus of an article in a trade magazine.

Design Firm: Sayles Graphic Design
Art Director/Designer: John Sayles
Illustrator: John Sayles
Client: Central Life Assurance

1

1 This piece reintroduced a paper that had been improved and updated with a more contemporary color palette. It includes extensive production notes for its audience of designers and printers. "It was intended to be an idea generator, but also an educational tool," says Paul Wharton of LIttle & Company.

Design Firm: Little & Company
Art Director/Designer: Mike Lizama
Copywriter: Sandra Bucholtz
Client: Cross Pointe Paper Corp.

ART INSTITUTE OF ATLANTA
LIBRARY

1

1 Titled "Passport to Russia," this paper promotion introduced a new finish for an established line and demonstrates a variety of printing techniques. "We also tried to reinforce the product name by using travel as a theme," says its art director and designer Paul Wharton.

Design Firm: Little & Company
Art Director/Designer: Paul Wharton
Copywriter: Sandra Bucholtz
Client: Cross Pointe Paper Corp.

1

2

1 "The sweetest way to attract prospects" is what this telephone media company promises its prospective clients. This clever promotion got attention and delivered results: a direct return of 35 percent responded to the 800 number provided.

Design Firm: DBD International, Ltd.
Art Director/Designer: David Brier
Client: Phoneworks

2 A similar promotion for the same client, which included a bottle of hot sauce, yielded a return of 30 percent.

Design Firm: DBD International, Ltd.
Art Director/Designer: David Brier
Client: Phoneworks

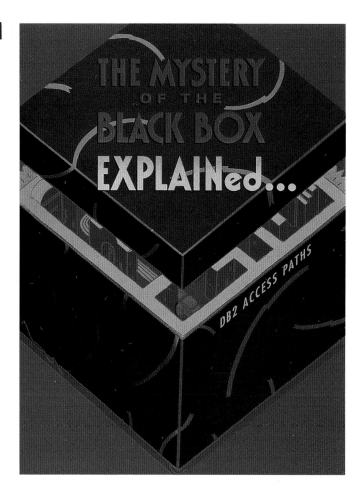

1

2

1 This intriguing postcard depicts a partially opened box containing a maze. "The client wanted to build a qualified list for a new product with this mailing," says Grafik Communications's Cheryl Clark. Those who responded to the postcard mailing received an informational follow-up mailing that included a poster of a maze.

Design Firm: Grafik Communications, Ltd.
Design Team Members: Gregg Glaviano, Judy Kirpich, Susan English
Illustrator: Bill Mayer
Client: Systems Center, Inc.

2 A series of postcards "from the edge of the UNIX network" hinted at the client's ability to solve systems problems. Many recipients got such a kick out of the series they contacted the client requesting additional cards to share with industry colleagues.

Design Firm: Grafik Communications, Ltd.
Design Team Members: Richard Hamilton, Judy Kirpich
Illustrator: Kim Pope
Client: Systems Center, Inc.

1 Promoting a new line of environmentally friendly mailers presented a golden opportunity for playing up the elegant printability of their brown Kraft surface. A design solution employing metallic inks on the mailer and its promotional brochure made the most of this new product's design potential.

Design Firm: Brand Design Company
Art Director: Andy Cruz
Designer: Andy Cruz, Rich Roat, Allen Mercer
Photographer: Carlos Alejandro
Client: Calumet Carton Company

2 Recipients of this brochure were intrigued with the packet of sunflower seeds that was affixed to its cover. Significant numbers of networking software users responded to the client's offer to trade in their old software for their program.

Design Firm: Dickinson Associates
Art Director/Designer: Marc English
Illustrator: James Kraus
Client: Sun Select

1

2

1 This box of promotional items was conceived to help market a new line of office furniture. It delivered, generating a significant number of leads for the client's sales force.

Design Firm: Nancy Yerkes Design
Art Director/Designer: Nancy Yerkes
Client: Herman Miller, Inc.

2 When a printing company decided to expand its business as a turn-key provider of software, a brochure was needed to explain the business to prospective clients. The brochure contributed to the huge success of this venture which, according to designer Jack Anderson, has now eclipsed its parent company.

Design Firm: Hornall Anderson Design Works
Art Director: Jack Anderson, Heidi Hatlestad
Designer: Bruce Branson-Meyer
Client: Six Sigma

1

1 This promotional brochure explains the de-inking process as part of making recycled stock. "We wanted to show the process as easily as we could," says the brochure's art director Paul Wharton. The brochure, and its accompanying poster, have also gained additional exposure through their use in schools.

Design Firm: Little & Company
Art Director: Paul Wharton
Designer: Jason Reynolds
Illustrator: Phillippe Weisbecker
Copywriter: Words At Work
Client: Cross Pointe Paper Corp.

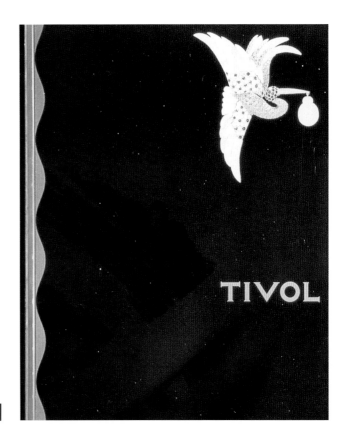

1

2

1 An upscale look that made the most of the client's product line was the most appropriate choice for the cover of this mail-order catalog. According to Muller & Company's creative director, a record 25 percent of the client's sales came directly from this catalog.

Design Firm: Muller & Company
Art Director/Designer: John Muller
Photographer: Mike Regnier
Client: Tivol

2 "The goal of this piece was to position the client as the leader in the industry," says its designer and art director Jack Anderson. This sophisticated catalog was produced in three different languages and succeeded in marketing the client's products on a multicultural level.

Design Firm: Hornall Anderson Design Works
Art Director: Jack Anderson
Designer: Jack Anderson, David Bates, Mary Chin Hutchison
Photographer: Jim Cummins, Various
Illustrator: Todd Connor, Yutaka Sasaki
Client: Giro Sport Design, Inc.

1

2

1 This mailing was sent to cosmetic manufacturers to introduce a new packaging option, "The Pinnacle."

Design Firm: Sayles Graphic Design
Art Director/Designer: John Sayles
Illustrator: John Sayles
Client: Berlin Packaging

2 Costs were kept to a minimum on this promotion for a systems management product. Its press run was limited to two colors to reserve the production budget for intriguing diecuts and special folds that made the most of its tongue-in-cheek play on the dictionary.

Design Firm: Grafik Communications, Ltd.
Design Team Members: Jennifer Johnson
Judy Kirpich
Illustrator: Jennifer Johnson
Client: Systems Center, Inc.

1 A new name and new identity for an existing store chain required a reintroduction in the form of a series of postcards. Mailed on a weekly basis, each postcard featured a section of the market.

Design Firm: Hornall Anderson Design Works
Art Director: Jack Anderson
Designer: Jack Anderson, Julie Tanagi-Lock
Illustrator: Hornall Anderson Design Works
Client: Tradewell

2 A new product unveiling marked a special occasion for this promotional package.

Design Firm: Hornall Anderson Design Works
Art Director: Jack Anderson
Designer: Jack Anderson, Julie Tanagi-Lock, Denise Weir
Illustrator: Scott McDougall
Client: Asymetrix Corporation

1

2

1 This direct mail piece contained 27 different kinds of coated papers, printed with the same image so that designers and paper buyers could compare and contrast samples. Its donut theme provided a clever way to show off the paper's diecutting capabilities.

Design Firm: Supon Design Group, Inc.
Creative Director: Supon Phornirunlit
Art Director/Designer: Andrew Dolan
Photographer: Earl Zubkoff
Client: Frank Parsons Paper Company

2 Markets for newspaper subscribers include hotels which deliver the morning paper to their guests. This promotional package, consisting of three brochures and a cover letter, promoted *The Washington Post* to hotel managers in the Washington D.C. area.

Design Firm: Supon Design Group, Inc.
Creative Director: Supon Phornirunlit
Art Director: Andrew Dolan
Designer: Richard Boynton, Apisak Saibua
Photographer: Barry Myers
Client: *The Washington Post*

1

1 This piece relies on a look of what Europeans revere as "Americana," a '50s retro-look, to promote a trendy new clothing shop in Italy.

Design Firm: Metalli Lindberg Adv
Art Director/Designer: Lionello Borean, Stefano Dal Tin
Client: Tirindelli Clothes Shop

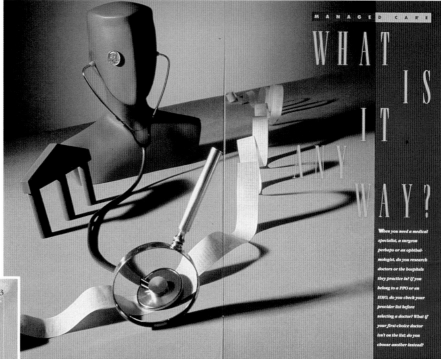

1 A Midwestern medical center did a mass mailing of this brochure to donors, employees, and the general public. Published on a quarterly basis, the brochure continues to be a useful resource for its recipients—generating good will while, at the same time, promoting hospital services and staff.

Design Firm: Rickabaugh Graphics
Art Director/Designer: Eric Rickabaugh
Photographer: Larry Hamill
Illustrator: Michael Linley
Client: Grant Medical Center

2 This promotional mailer for a paper mill shows how much impact a one-color piece can have when printed on the paper line it promotes. The components of the mailing included a jigsaw puzzle, brochure, and a "lucky charm" keepsake.

Design Firm: Sayles Graphic Design
Art Director/Designer: John Sayles
Illustrator: John Sayles
Client: Gilbert Paper

1 To introduce a line of cookies, this brochure was mailed nationally to over 20,000 retailers and wholesalers. "This brochure boosted their sales quite a bit," says its designer, Damion Hickman.

Design Firm: Mac By Night Design
Art Director/Designer: Damion Hickman, Hector Garcia
Photographer: Scott Montgomery
Illustrator: Damion Hickman
Client: Bakery Street Cookie Company

2 This pewterware manufacturer wanted to project an upscale image on a limited budget. Their mail order catalog achieves its rich, understated look with full-color product shots and subtle graphics.

Design Firm: Whitney•Edwards Design
Art Director: Charlene Whitney Edwards
Designer: Barbara Christopher
Photographer: Richard Dorbin, Paragon Light
Illustrator: Charlene Edwards
Client: Salisbury Pewter

GUARANTEED ACCURACY

ginny's DOCUMENTARY
A document handling service for attorneys.

ACCURACY is the name of the game in your business and in ours. We back that up with our unconditional guarantee. CALL 478-RUSH.

YOU MAKE THE CASE, WE'LL MAKE THE COPIES.

■

CASE CLOSED.

The **OBVIOUS CHOICE** for all your legal document handling? Ginny's Documentary. Why? Guaranteed accuracy; fast

ginny's DOCUMENTARY
A document handling service for attorneys.

professional service; wide range of capabilities; free pick-up & delivery, secure facilities. **CASE CLOSED.** CALL 478-RUSH.

THE TRUTH, THE WHOLE TRUTH & NOTHING BUT THE TRUTH . . .

ginny's DOCUMENTARY
A document handling service for attorneys.

We keep our **COMMITMENTS.** Guaranteed. We're fast, accurate, and convenient. When you need legal copying work, CALL 478-RUSH.

WE'LL LOSE SLEEP SO YOU WON'T HAVE TO

YOU MAKE THE CASE, WE'LL MAKE THE COPIES

ginny's DOCUMENTARY
A document handling service for attorneys.

CALL 478-RUSH.

YOU specialize in the law. **WE** specialize in legal copying. Professional client representatives are available to serve your needs. We're fast, accurate, and offer free pickup & delivery.

WE'LL LOSE SLEEP SO YOU WON'T HAVE TO.

■ "It's really important in the legal documentary business to keep your firm's name in front of your clients," says Tracy Grubs, the designer of this postcard series. Mailed to over 5,000 lawyers at two-week intervals, this series of cards helped to put this new business venture on the map.

Design Firm: Aslan Grafix
Art Director/Designer: Tracy Grubbs
Client: Ginny's Documentary

1 This moving announcement for a lighting company carried the client's new business card. It was mailed in an oversized, custom envelope, imprinted with the client's logo and a teaser.

Design Firm: Sayles Graphic Design
Art Director/Designer: John Sayles
Illustrator: John Sayles
Client: Adventure Lighting

2 The need for a budget-conscious approach dictated the format for this self-mailer. It was printed on a single 8 ¹/₂ x 11 sheet and folded to a 8 ¹/₂ x 5 ¹/₂ inch brochure. The opposite side carried postage and an address label.

Design Firm: Bennett Peji Design
Art Director/Designer: Bennett Peji
Illustrator: Bennett Peji
Client: Scotland Concerts

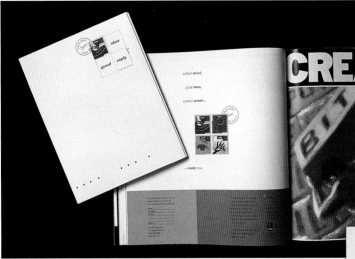

1

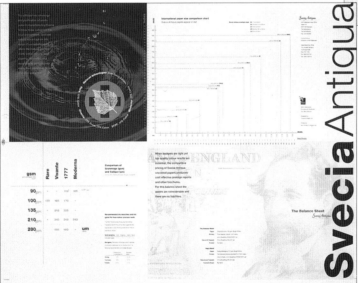

1 This paper promotion, mailed to designers and printers all over Great Britain, took full advantage of the postage area to reiterate the message within.

Design Firm: Trickett & Webb Limited
Art Director: Lynn Trickett, Brian Webb
Designer: Colin Gifford, Avril Bradley
Photographer/Illustrator: Trickett & Webb Limited
Client: Svecia Antiqua Papers

1

2

1 This sales brochure for a pharmaceutical firm needed to project a distinctive image. "It's a very competitive field," says designer Daniel Michael Flynn of the drug industry. "We gave it a look that made it stand out from the competition." The brochure coordinates with a follow-up binder containing product information.

Design Firm: Vaughn Wedeen Creative
Art Director: Rick Vaughn, Daniel Michael Flynn
Designer: Daniel Michael Flynn
Client: National Institutional Pharamacy Services, Inc.

2 This capabilities brochure featured the intriguing work of artist M.C. Escher, to get across its message of problem solving. Its use of art in the public domain also cost less than a commissioned illustration.

Design Firm: Lebowitz Gould Design, Inc.
Art Director: Susan Chait, Sue Gould
Designer: Susan Chait
Client: Molino & Associates, Inc./BAI

3 (Opposite page) Showcasing this printer's capability required a multicomponent mailer that included a poster, an indentifier and gift card. The mailing was sent to current and potential clients.

Design Firm: Janet Hughes and Associates
Art Director/Designer: Donna Perzel
Photographer: Stephen Hone
Calligrapher: Paul DeCampli
Client: Phototype Color Graphics

1

I This seaside inn wanted a new brochure to promote its recent remodeling. "We also had to project a feeling of tradition," says its designer Charlene Whitney Edwards. "We couldn't be tempted by current design trends."

Design Firm: Whitney•Edwards Design
Art Director: Charlene Whitney Edwards
Designer: Barbara Christopher
Photographer: J. Tyler Campbell
Client: The Tidewater Inn

1 This series of direct mail catalogs for an antique dealer achieved consistency through a standard format and similar color treatment.

Design Firm: Trickett & Webb Limited
Art Director: Lynn Trickett, Brian Webb
Designer: Lynn Trickett
Client: Rennies

2 A cardboard suitcase with a railroad travel theme housed samples of the client's product: screen-printed T-shirts. The suitcase was mailed to prospective customers without an outer wrapper. An area on the top was reserved for the address label and postage.

Design Firm: Sayles Graphic Design
Art Director/Designer: John Sayles
Illustrator: John Sayles
Client: Logo-Motive

1

1 Printing photos of a computer keyboard in bright, solarized colors yielded a dramatic, eye-catching effect for this direct mail piece which promoted a marketing research firm.

Design Firm: Trickett & Webb Limited
Art Director: Lynn Trickett, Brian Webb
Designer: Steve Edwards
Photographer: Zafar Baron
Client: Research Resources

1 A newly established service bureau benefited immensely from this introductory mailer. According to its designer, Fred Tieken, an initial mailing of 4,000 generated an unexpected surge of new business for the client.

Design Firm: Tieken Design and Creative Services
Art Director/Designer: Fred E. Tieken
Photographer: Rick Gayle
Client: ImageLab

THERE'S A FAMOUS MUSEUM
IN SAN ANTONIO WHERE A LONG LIST OF
OUTSTANDING ARTISTS RESIDES.

Kindly accept our invitation to a private tour during the NFRA Meeting in April. You are invited to be the guest of DuPont on Tuesday, April 3 for a special tour and brunch at the distinguished McNay Art Museum in San Antonio.

As your host for the day, we have made all the arrangements for you. A continental breakfast will be served at 9 a.m. in Section C of the Ballroom at the Marriott Rivercenter Hotel. The coach will then depart for the museum at 10 a.m. Brunch will be served in the Sculpture Garden at the conclusion of the viewing and local artist Jay Hester will speak. Arrival back at the hotel will be approximately 2 p.m.

Meet artist Jay Hester, our guest speaker at brunch. A renowned sculptor and painter whose works have been collected and exhibited throughout the South, Jay Hester resides in the scenic Hill Country of Texas. He has sculpted works in a variety of media—from bronze to clay—and has painted in watercolors, acrylics and oils. Most known for his ceramics and oil-paint portraits, this gifted artist will inform and inspire us with his passion for his work.

After your tour, this will frame a fine piece of art. We will be pleased to present you with a gift print from the McNay collection of originals, following your visit to the museum. You may save this frame and use it to display the print at home.

We hope you will be our guest for a day at the McNay. One of the few places you'll find so many great artists' paintings in residence.

Mark your confirmation card and mail it in the enclosed envelope by March 12.

WHAT'S THE
ONE PLACE
WHERE ALL
THESE
GREAT NAMES
APPEAR
TOGETHER?

Watercolor on paper
The Mary and Sylvan Lang Collection
Marion Koogler McNay Art Museum
San Antonio, Texas

GIRL ON A GARDEN SEAT
(WOMAN SEATED ON BENCH) 1878

Winslow Homer
American, 1836-1910

FUNDRAISING AND RECRUITING

1 When this piece is opened a hand-assembled cardboard football assembles itself from a flattened position and pops up and into the air to a height of up to ten feet. The piece got a great response from its alumni audience who attended Alumni Weekend in record-breaking numbers.

Design Firm: Love Packaging Group
Art Director/Designer: Brian Miller
Illustrator: Brian Miller
Client: Wichita Collegiate School

2 A clear plastic mailing tube contains this brochure about the Buena Vista College "Point of View." The components of this mailer also include a working kaleidoscope which, when viewed, shows the Buena Vista logo.

Design Firm: Sayles Graphic Design
Art Director/Designer: John Sayles
Illustrator: John Sayles
Client: Buena Vista College

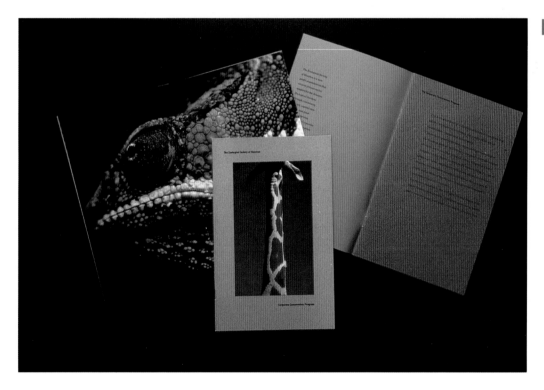

1 The goal of this direct-mail booklet was to generate attendance for performances of a contemporary dance company. It achieved its avant-garde look with a limited budget, two-color approach.

Design Firm: Moore Moscowitz
Art Director: Jan Moscowitz
Designer: Tim Moore
Client: Dance Umbrella

2 The Zoological Society of Houston is a nonprofit organization that secures private-sector support for the Houston Zoological Gardens through community appeals, capital campaigns, and fundraising programs. This brochure outlines the benefits of the Corporate Conservators Program.

Design Firm: Lowell Williams Design, Inc.
Art Director/Designer: Lana Rigsby
Photographer: Arthur Meyerson
Client: Zoological Society of Houston

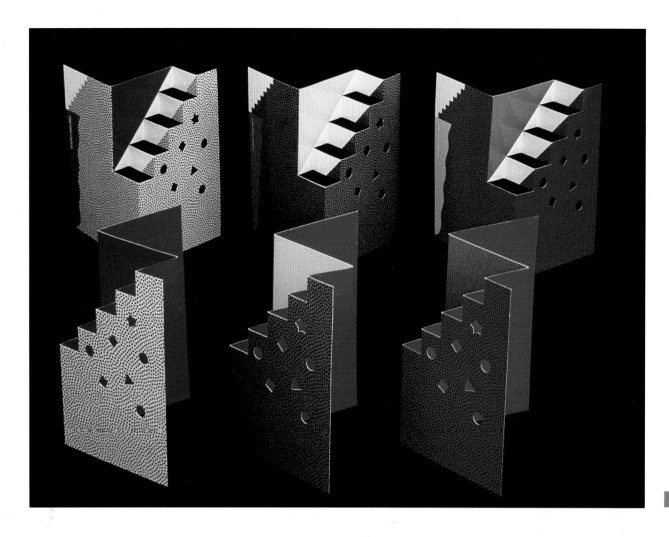

1

2

1 These cards were commissioned by the Moca-Museum of Contemporary Art as a fundraiser. The design served a dual purpose. With revised interior copy, they functioned as a self-promotional holiday mailing for Shimokochi/Reeves.

Design Firm: Shimokochi/Reeves
Art Director/Designer: Mamoru Shimokochi, Anne Reeves
Client: Moca-Museum of Contemporary Art, Shiokochi/Reeves

2 A brightly colored box houses three-dimensional graphics visible through an acetate window. Inside is a tiny, one-inch-square brochure giving details of the promoted event.

Design Firm: Sayles Graphic Design
Art Director/Designer: John Sayles
Illustrator: John Sayles
Client: University of California, Santa Barbara

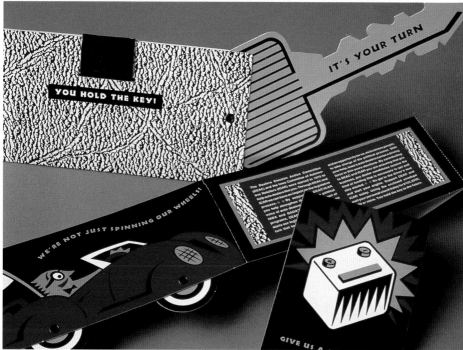

1 A hinged key swivels out of this self-mailer which also contains a brochure. The spinning wheels on the car invited interaction with curious recipients who responded to this recruitment tool in record numbers.

Design Firm: Sayles Graphic Design
Art Director/Designer: John Sayles
Illustrator: John Sayles
Client: Iowa Automobile Dealers Association

2 This eye-catching poster, printed in two distinctive color combinations, is sent to secondary schools all over the country. Principal Mark Schwartz says it resulted in a 67 percent increase in inquiries from prospective students.

Design Firm: Nesnadny + Schwartz
Art Director: Joyce Nesnadny, Mark Schwartz
Designers: Joyce Nesnadny, Michelle Moehler
Photographer: Robert Muller, Tony Festa
Client: Cleveland Institute of Art

1 This brochure, promoting season tickets for the New Mexico Symphony Orchestra, uses two colors to keep costs down. Each layer of graphic elements represented a different aspect of the season's concerts.

Design Firm: Vaughn Wedeen Creative
Art Director: Steve Wedeen
Designers: Daniel Michael Flynn, Steve Wedeen
Client: New Mexico Symphony Orchestra

2 (Opposite page) This multicomponent mailer, promoting a museum tour and brunch, was mailed with a gold frame. Those who attended the tour received a print to fit their frame.

Design Firm: Janet Hughes and Associates
Art Director/Designer: Donna Perzel
Client: Du Pont

THERE'S A FAMOUS MUSEUM IN SAN ANTONIO WHERE A LONG LIST OF OUTSTANDING ARTISTS RESIDES.

Kindly accept our invitation to a private tour during the NBPA Meeting in April. You are invited to be the guest of DuPont on Tuesday, April 3 for a special tour and brunch at the distinguished McNay Art Museum in San Antonio.

As your host for the day, we have made all the arrangements for you. A continental breakfast will be served at 9 a.m. in Section C of the Ballroom at the Marriott Rivercenter Hotel. The coach will then depart for the museum at 10 a.m. Brunch will be served in the Sculpture Garden at the conclusion of the viewing and local artist Jay Hester will speak. Arrival back at the hotel will be approximately 2 p.m.

Meet artist Jay Hester, our guest speaker at brunch. A renowned sculptor and painter whose works have been collected and exhibited throughout the South, Jay Hester resides in the scenic Hill Country of Texas. He has sculpted works in a variety of media — from bronze to clay — and has painted in watercolors, acrylics and oils. Most known for his ceramics and oil-paint portraits, this gifted artist will inform and inspire us with his passion for his work.

After your tour, this will frame a fine piece of art. We will be pleased to present you with a gift print from the McNay collection of originals, following your visit to the museum. You may save this frame and use it to display the print at home.

We hope you will be our guest for a day at the McNay. One of the few places you'll find so many great artists' paintings in residence.

Mark your confirmation card and mail it in the enclosed envelope by March 12.

WHAT'S THE
ONE PLACE WHERE ALL THESE
GREAT NAMES APPEAR
TOGETHER?

Gift
To:
you

Watercolor on paper
The Marie and Sylvan Lang Collection
Marion Koogler McNay Art Museum
San Antonio, Texas

GIRL ON A GARDEN SEAT
(WOMAN SEATED ON BENCH) 1878

Winslow Homer
American, 1836-1910

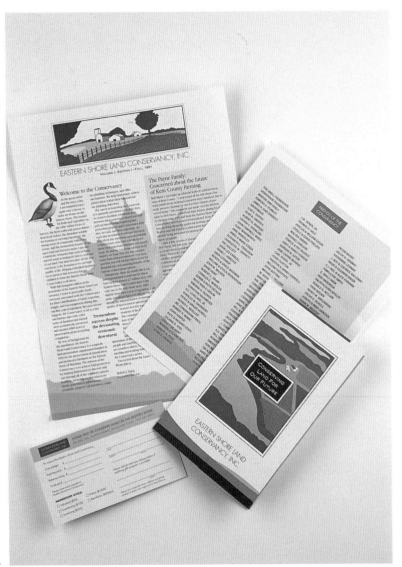

1 This brochure tells junior high school students to "Chart Your Course" to Dowling High School. It folds out to reveal a working compass.

Design Firm: Sayles Graphic Design
Art Director/Designer: John Sayles
Illustrator: John Sayles
Client: Dowling High School

2 Used as a fundraiser for a conservation group, this direct mail brochure achieves an environmentally friendly look with just two colors. According to its designer, Charlene Whitney Edwards, the client had a hard time keeping up with the response it generated.

Design Firm: Whitney-Edwards Design
Art Director: Charlene Whitney Edwards
Designer: Barbara Christopher, Charlene Edwards
Client: Eastern Shore Land Conservancy

I This two-part mailing, seeking corporate sponsors for the NYZS Wildlife Conservation Society, consisted of a teaser (top) followed by an informational brochure a few days later. According to the Society, follow-up phone calls indicated that most of the mailing's recipients remembered it.

Design Firm: Parham Santana Inc.
Art Director: John Parham
Designer: Okey B. Westor
Client: NYZS Wildlife Conservation Society

1 This brochure promotes an annual fundraiser with travel as its theme. Its designer, Lana Rigsby, used rare stamps borrowed from a local collector as a visual theme. Rigsby says the piece drew a large crowd: "Attendance was up 20 percent over the prior year," she reports.

Design Firm: Rigsby Design, Inc.
Art Director/Designer: Lana Rigsby
Illustrator: Lana Rigsby, Deborah Brochstein
Client: Alley Theatre, Houston

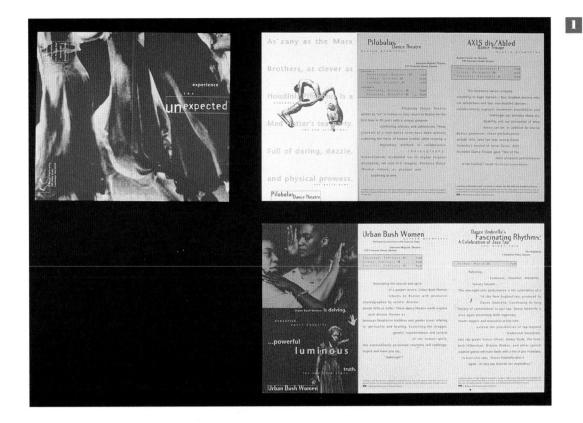

1 This dance company wanted a contemporary, upscale promotional mailer on a two-color budget. The piece achieves its multicolored look through the use of colored stock.

Design Firm: Moore Moscowitz
Art Director: Jan Moscowitz
Designer: Tim Moore
Client: Dance Umbrella

2 A number of different fundraising events, all benefiting a museum, were described in this mailer. Each of the cards represents a single event.

Design Firm: Muller & Company
Art Director: John Muller
Designer: Peter Corcoran
Illustrator: Peter Corcoran
Client: The Nelson-Atkins Museum of Art

1 This two-part mailing of coordinated pieces promoted an art auction benefiting the Mental Health Association of South Central Kansas. The "call for art" off-size brochure (left) mailed in its own, tailored-to-size box, generated a large number of artistic contributions. The mailer announcing the auction (at right) is attached to a bidding paddle with a twine hand strap. According to art director Tracy Holdeman, the auction was extremely successful, raising over $10,000.

Design Firm: Love Packaging Group
Art Director: Tracy Holdeman
Designer: Tracy Holdeman, Brian Miller
Client: Mental Health Association of South Central Kansas

2 This ribbon-bound booklet is actually an invitation to a Victorian Christmas party to benefit a children's home in Dallas. Attendees were asked to bring a gift for a child. The piece was so successful that "We had seven truckloads of gifts to take to the home," says art director Lyn Johnson.

Design Firm: Buchanan Printing Co.
Art Director: Lyn Johnson
Designer: Mark M. Bedell
Illustrator: Mark M. Bedel
Client: Buchanan Printing

1 A combination direct-mail brochure and poster, this multilayered mailer arrives in a chipboard "book jacket." As the piece is read, it unfolds to reveal a poster and its "Success by the Book" theme.

Design Firm: Sayles Graphic Design
Art Director/Designer: John Sayles
Illustrator: John Sayles
Client: University of California, Santa Barbara

2 This brochure was sent to season ticket holders and potential NMSO Symphony subscribers. "The brochures worked well for the client, averaging a 10% response," says Vaughn Wedeen principal, Richard Kuhn.

Design Firm: Vaughn Wedeen Creative
Art Director: Steve Wedeen
Designer: Daniel Michael Flynn
Client: New Mexico Symphony Orchestra

SELF-PROMOTION

1

2

1 Slides of portfolio samples masquerade as tea bags in this clever promotional strategy. Sent to prospective clients as an introductory promotion, "it was really well received," says the firm's account executive Christine Bassi.

Design Firm: Design Horizons International
Art Director: Bryan Sanzotti
Designer: Janan Cain
Photographer: Aldus Sauley
Illustrator: Janan Cain
Client Design Horizons International

2 A collaborative promotional effort by a group of illustrators yielded this unusual deck of playing cards. Each card shows an illustration sample on one side, and has the illustrator's name, address, and phone number on the reverse.

Design Firm: Mires Design, Inc.
Art Director/Designer: José Serrano
Illustrator: Jennifer Hewitson
Client: Joined At The Hip

3 (Opposite page) Unfamiliar events were depicted in this monthly series of calendar promotions. "To defray my costs, I shared expenses with the photographer and stylist," says its designer Derek Dalton. Personal imprints were done as a separate press run for each collaborator.

Design Firm: Derek Dalton Design
Art Director/Designer: Derek Dalton
Photographer: Fred Slavin
Stylist: Phyllis Frazier
Client: Derek Dalton, Phyllis Frazier, Fred Slavin

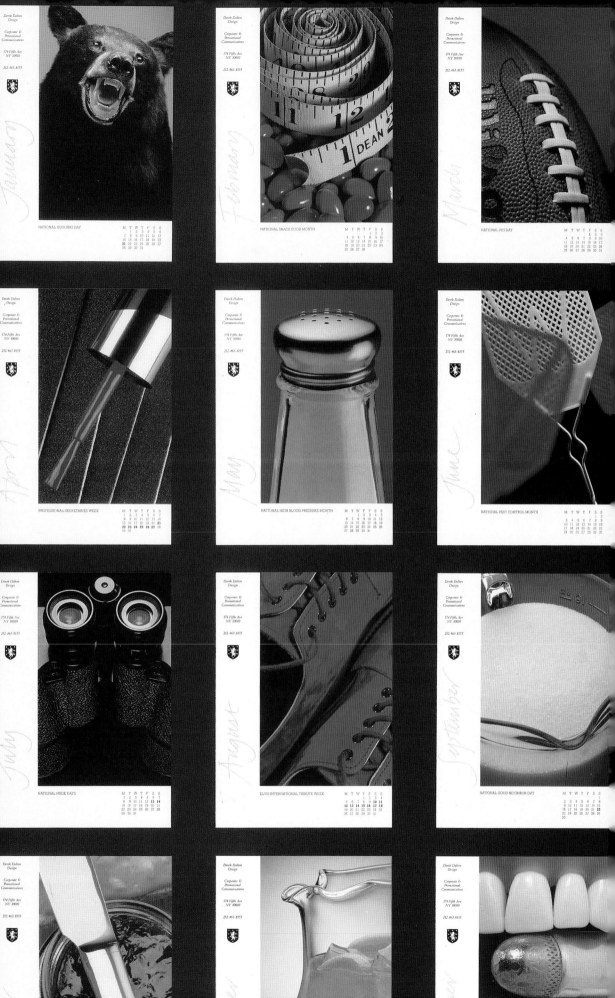
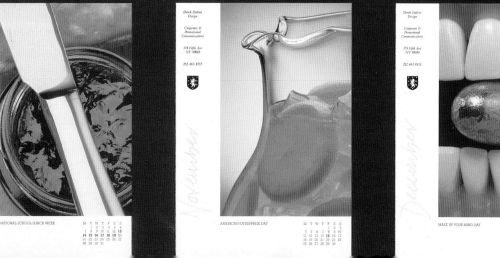

1 As a holiday promotional piece and thank-you gift, Abrams Design sent a carton of color-coordinated surprise boxes to its clients—one box for each of the 12 days of Christmas. Each box contained a holiday ornament, confection, or keepsake.

Design Firm: Abrams Design Group
Art Director: Colleen Abrams
Designer: Colleen Abrams, Kari Perin, Kay Watanabe
Client: Abrams Design Group

2 For a charming, hand-crafted look, this book of holiday lore was produced entirely on a letterpress and bound by hand. It was sent to clients, vendors, and friends as a seasonal greeting.

Design Firm: Rickabaugh Graphics
Art Director: Eric Rickabaugh
Designer: Michael Tennyson Smith
Illustrator: Michael Tennyson Smith
Client: Rickabaugh Graphics

1

2

1 This book of seasonal imagery and verse was a collaboration between a printer, photographer, and design studio. All parties sent the piece as a holiday self-promotion to current and prospective clients.

Design Firm: Lamson Design
Art Director/Designer: Dale Lamson
Photographer: Greg Grosse
Client: Lamson Design

2 A move from Apple Street to Grape Street prompted this design firm to send bottles of apple wine and burgundy to its clients. A map, new phone number reminder card, and an invitation to an open house were included. "Two hundred plus clients and friends joined us in a wonderful evening of food, fun, and vintage," says firm principal Gil Hanson.

Design Firm: Hanson Associates, inc.
Art Director: Gil Hanson
Designer: Deborah McSorley
Illustrator: Deborah McSorley
Client: Hanson Associates, inc.

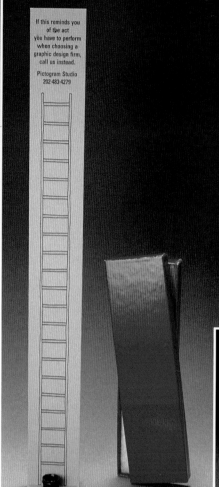

I Each of the boxes in this promotional series was sent to a prospective client every two to three weeks. "They've really helped us break the ice with new clients," says firm principal Stephanie Hooton.

Design Firm: Pictogram Studio
Art Director: Hien Nguyen
Designer: Hien Nguyen, Stephanie Hooton
Client: Pictogram Studio

1 This moving announcement emphasizes its "packing up" message by using boxes as props in a series of staff photos. The box theme is reinforced by its corrugated outer mailer.

Design Firm: Mires Design, Inc.
Art Director/Designer: Scott Mires
Photographer: Chris Wimpey
Client: Mires Design, Inc.

1 (This page and opposite) Three Fish Design decided to play up its name with a holiday gift to clients of fish-shaped ornaments. Sent every year for the past four holiday seasons, the ornaments keep the firm's name in the minds of clients. "Our clients really enjoy receiving a different ornament each year and look forward to what the next year will be," says art director Cynthia Henry. Ornaments from a past holiday mailing have also served as an enclosure for follow-up thank-you notes to prospective clients after a portfolio showing.

Design Firm: Three Fish Design
Art Director: Caroline Vaaler, Cynthia Henry
Designer: Caroline Vaaler
Client: Three Fish Design

three fish design
3538 Fremont Avenue South
Minneapolis, Minnesota 55408

Terri
55441
C

Thanks for taking the time to review our portfolio.
I enjoyed meeting with you, and look forward to the Possibility of working with you soon.

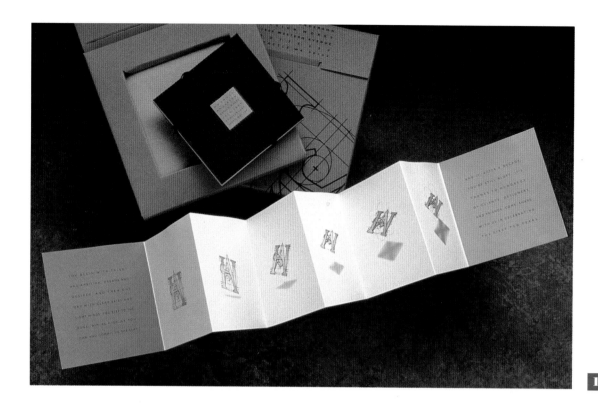

1 Hornall Anderson's 10th anniversary marked the occasion for a special self-promotion campaign. The firm did a mailing to clients and friends announcing its anniversary and a party marking the occasion at the Seattle Flight Museum.

Design Firm: Hornall Anderson Design Works
Art Director: Jack Anderson
Designer: Jack Anderson, David Bates, Lian Ng
Illustrator: Yutaka Sasaki
Client: Hornall Anderson Design Works

2 At its anniversary party the design firm gave this special commemorative book to those who attended. It documented the firm's progress over its 10-year history.

Design Firm: Hornall Anderson Design Works
Art Director: Jack Anderson
Designer: Jack Anderson, David Bates, Lian Ng
Illustrator: Yutaka Sasaki
Client: Hornall Anderson Design Works

1 Hanson Associates chose a promotional mailing of a custom-packaged food item as a client gift. "A nicely designed package with our name on it can remain in a customer's kitchen and memory for a long time," says firm principal Gil Hanson.

Design Firm: Hanson Associates, inc.
Art Director: Gil Hanson
Designer: Christy Verna
Illustrator: Christy Verna
Client: Hanson Associates, inc.

2 This promotional mailing was sent to a list of approximately 3,000 prospective clients in the New York City area. It generated close to 300 inquiries from the business reply card included.

Design Firm: DBD International
Art Director/Designer: David Brier
Client: DBD International

3 This signed and numbered, limited edition serigraph did double duty as a client gift for the holidays and to showcase the artistic ability of its designer.

Design Firm: Puccinelli Design
Art Director: Keith Puccinelli
Designer: Keith Puccinelli, Heidi Palladino
Illustrator: Keith Puccinelli
Client: Puccinelli Design

1 This promotion's distinctive odor was hard for its recipients to ignore. "Our office was scented for an entire month after we worked with more than 800 of these fresheners," says principal Maruchi Santana. "But clients remember this piece as one of our most creative promotions."

Design Firm: Parham Santana
Art Directors: Maruchi Santana, John Parham
Designer: Maruchi Santana
Copywriter: Mary Louise Chatel

2 This piece's use of pop-up hands catches attention and reinforces its promotion of a hand lettering service. In response to this clever piece, "We got plenty of inquiries," says firm principal Ivan Angelic.

Design Firm: Hoffmann & Angelic Design
Art Director: Ivan Angelic
Designer: Andrea Hoffman
Calligrapher: Ivan Angelic
Client: Hoffmann & Angelic Design

3 This series of six oversized postcards (opposite page) was conceived to promote a variety of design approaches. They were mailed over a two-month period. "My follow up calls immediately indicated a positive response to the mailings," says Monderer.

Design Firm: Stewart Monderer Design, Inc.
Art Director: Stewart Monderer
Designers: Robert Davison, Jane Winsor
Illustrator: Richard Goldberg
Client: Stewart Monderer Design, Inc.

1

2

1 As a holiday greeting, Pentagram sent out this cookbook filled with charming recipes written by kindergarteners.

Design Firm: Pentagram
Art Director: Michael Bierut
Designers: Michael Bierut, Agnethe Glatred
Illustrator: Eve Chwast
Client: Pentagram

2 Shimokochi/Reeves' distinctive logo has won many design awards and clients have often expressed their admiration of it. The firm sends out these distinctive lapel pins bearing its logo as a holiday greeting and followup gift for new clients.

Design Firm: Shimokochi/Reeves
Art Director/Designer: Mamoru Shimokochi, Anne Reeves
Client: Shimokochi/Reeves

3 The Christmas season has special meaning for the different members of Samata Associates' team. This holiday promotion gives each staffer an opportunity to share their seasonal sentiments.

Design Firm: Samata Associates
Art Director: Pat Samata
Designers: Pat Samata, Greg Samata
Photographer: Jean Moss
Illustrator: George Sawa
Client: Samata Associates

3

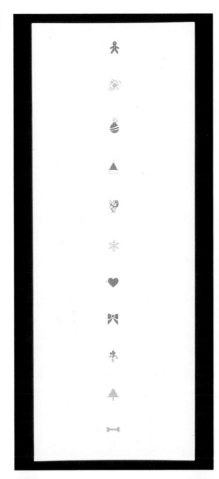

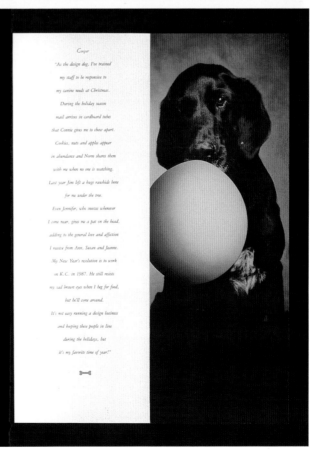

1

1 This well-coordinated promotional mailing, consisting of custom-packaged coffee, a greeting card, and special shipping boxes and labels, celebrates the Chinese Zodiac's Year of the Rooster. "We picked up a few clients and additional business from current ones as a result of this mailing," says firm principal Raymond Yu.

Design Firm: Pandamonium Designs
Art Director: Raymond Yu
Designers: Raymond Yu, Erin Kroninger
Photographer: Steven H. Lee
Client: Pandamonium Designs

2 Sent to clients and prospects as a holiday greeting, this animated, hand-assembled flip book shows the metamorphasis of a simple line sketch of a Christmas tree (at the opening) into a New Year's champagne glass (at the end). "People kept it," says designer Dan Howard. "It keeps our name in front of our clients."

Design Firm: Designsense
Designer: Dan Howard
Client: Designsense

3 This self-promotion artfully packages a variety of logo jobs. The distinctive outer mailer echoes the simplicity of its contents yet is eye-catching enough to catch a recipient's attention. "This promotional package put us on the map and helped me establish my business," says firm principal Carlos Segura.

Design Firm: Segura Inc.
Art Director/Designer: Carlos Segura
Illustrator: Carlos Segura
Client: Segura Inc.

1 A move to a new studio presents an opportunity for a promotional mailing. This piece's accordian folds and unique graphics encourage additional exposure as a stand-up display. "We've won numerous awards with it," says firm principal Anne Reeves, citing additional promotional mileage this recognition brought.

Design Firm: Shimokochi/Reeves
Art Director/Designer: Mamoru Shimokochi, Anne Reeves
Client: Shimokochi/Reeves

2 A message of holiday "Cheer" is literally depicted in this memorable promotion for a well-known photographer. "We wanted to promote him in a different way," says firm principal Forrest Richardson, who says this mailing stood out from the more mundane "portfolio" pieces photographers typically send out.

Design Firm: Richardson or Richardson
Art Director/Designer: Debi Young Mees
Copywriters: Valerie Richardson, Debi Young Mees
Client: Rick Gayle Studio Inc.

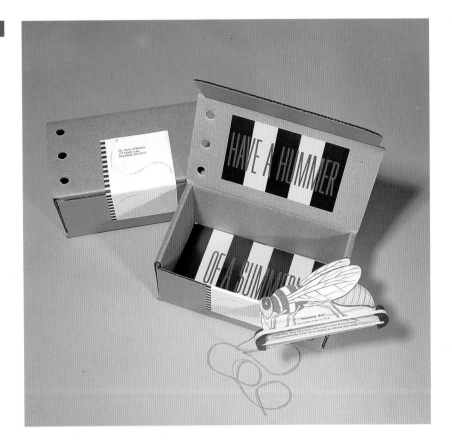

1 WYD traditionally sends an annual self-promotion with a summer theme to existing and prospective clients. This self-promotion includes a bee that actually hums when it's whirled overhead. Firm principal Frank Oswald says the piece generated goodwill and prompted many thank-you calls from clients. A year later, "We're still getting requests for bees," he says.

Design Firm: WYD Design, Inc.
Art Director: Randall Smith
Designer/Copywriter: Scott Kuykendall
Client: WYD Design, Inc.

2 The Golconda, a mythological creature Boelts Bros. created, serves as the basis for this promotional holiday mailing which includes a recounting of the Golconda legend and a ceramic miniature as a keepsake. "A fable was written," says principal Jackson Boelts, "and it was sent out in its own little wooden pen."

Design Firm: Boelts Bros. Design, Inc.
Art Director/Designer: Eric Boelts, Jackson Boelts, Kerry Stratford
Client: Boelts Bros. Design, Inc.

1

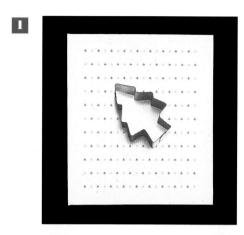

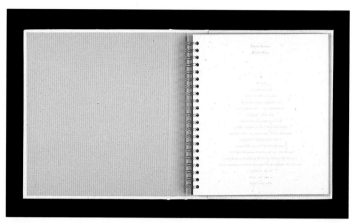

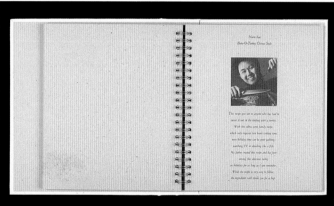

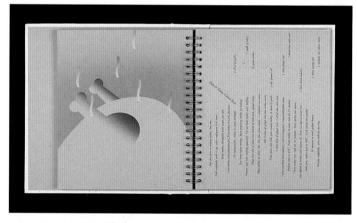

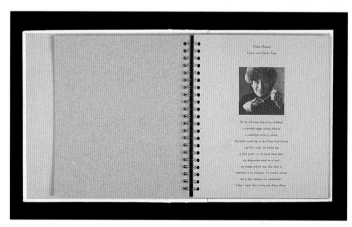

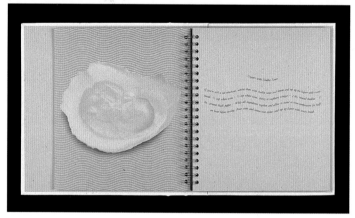

1 This stunning book of favorite recipes from Samata Associates is a holiday gift that serves as a year-round promotion to clients who frequently refer to it. Firm principal Pat Samata says clients have raved about many of the recipes they've tried.

Design Firm: Samata Associates
Art Director: Pat Samata
Designers: Pat Samata, Greg Samata
Photographer: Mark Joseph
Illustrator: Paul Thompson
Client: Samata Associates

2 Boelts Bros. offers their mom's great recipes in this holiday gift of a cookbook to prospective and existing clients. "Our mom is a terrific cook and we thought our clients would like her recipes as a holiday gift," says Jackson Boelts, adding that many are family recipes handed down over many generations.

Design Firm: Boelts Bros. Design, Inc.
Art Director/Designer: Eric Boelts, Jackson Boelts, Kerry Stratford
Client: Boelts Bros. Design, Inc.

3 This "rap wrap" for the holidays sends a clever promotional message to clients. The poster's display in the offices of its recipients brought Parham Santana additional exposure. "The piece gave us a lot of credibility in terms of our youth market exposure and was featured in the AIGA annual," says Maruchi Santana.

Design Firm: Parham Santana
Art Director: John Parham
Designer: Maruchi Santana
Copywriter: Mary Louise Chatel
Client: Parham Santana

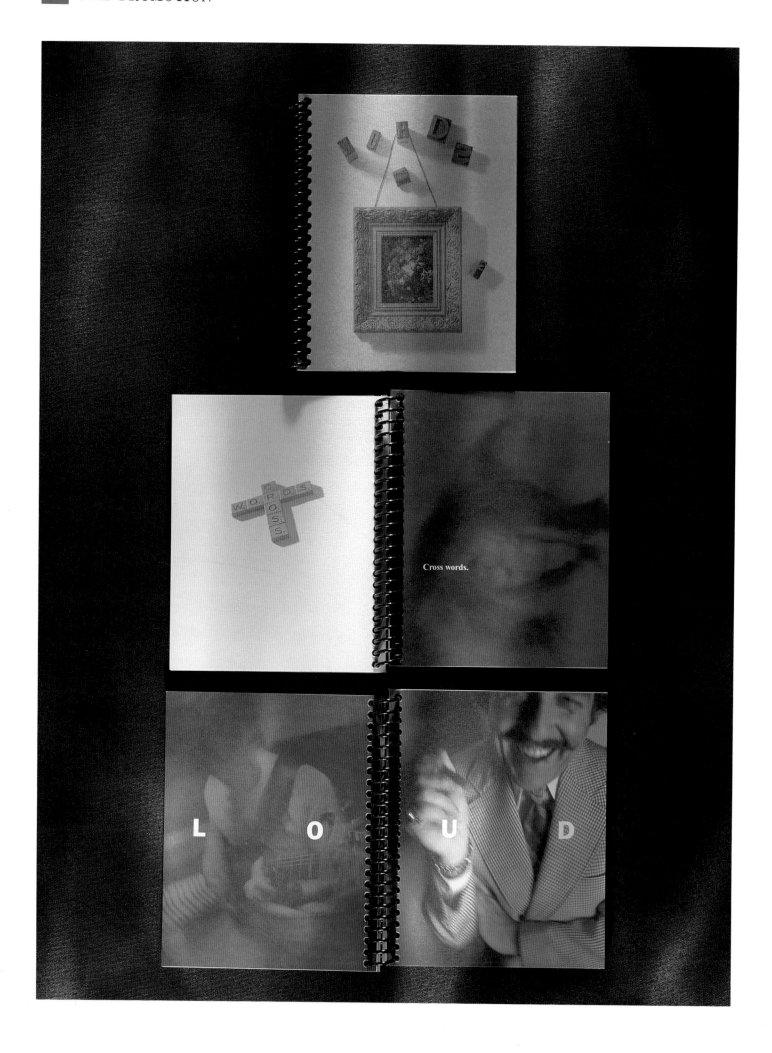

1 This self-promotional brochure (opposite) helped designer Cheryl Watson establish her new firm. Says Watson, "I show that there's more than one way to look at an idea. It serves as an example of my work and a promotion for prospective clients."

Design Firm: Graphiculture
Art Director/Designer: Cheryl Watson
Photographers: Marty Berglin, Neil Brown, Mark Gardner, Michael McCaffrey, Louise O'Brien, Daniel Schridde
Illustrators: Jane Mjolsness, Eric Hanson
Client: Graphiculture

2 This piece is one in a series of "tool" ornaments that Richardson or Richardson conceived for the firm. The promotional series has staying power. "They've all become collector's items," says Forrest Richardson.

Design Firm: Richardson or Richardson
Art Director: Ron Pannuzzo
Designer: Forrest Richardson
Copywriters: Valerie Richardson, Ron Pannuzzo
Client: Rowland Construction

3 This portfolio of package design samples has gone out to prospective clients in a distinctive self-mailer that serves, in itself, as an example of sophisticated package design.

Design Firm: Kollberg/Johnson Associates
Art Director: Penny Johnson
Designers: Arthur Wang, Michael Carr
Photographer: Jim Barber
Client: Kollberg/Johnson Associates

1

2

1 This printer's promotional mailer, sent out during the holidays, includes a card and gift of an appointment book. Foil stamping and lamination are among the various finishing techniques employed in the book's production.

Design Firm: Buchanan Printing
Art Director: Lyn Johnson
Designer/Illustrator: David Strand
Client: Buchanan Printing

2 A cooperative effort between printer and designer, this series of promotional mailings demonstrates a variety of printing techniques and design strategies. The series brought recognition to firm principal Jim Heins in the form of two ADDY awards and additional business. "It's been very effective for us," he says.

Design Firm: Heins Creative, Inc.
Art Director/Designer/Illustrator: Jim Heins
Client: Heins Creative, Inc., Fenske Printing

1

2

1 The 1992 Los Angeles Riots prompted Boelts Bros. to make a statement with this poster which was sent to its clients and friends.

Design Firm: Boelts Bros. Design
Art Director: Jackson Boelts, Dric Boelts
Client: Boelts Bros. Design

2 This custom-labeled and packaged wine does double duty demonstrating an effective packaging design strategy and generating good will as a client and vendor gift for the holidays.

Design Firm: Vaughn Wedeen Creative
Art Director: Steve Wedeen, Rick Vaughn
Designer/Illustrator: Daniel Michael Flynn
Client: Vaughn Wedeen Creative

1

2

1 This thought-provoking self-promotional brochure created for a writer elicited a response from many prospective clients who responded to its simple format and powerful imagery. The book also won several design awards, bringing recognition to designer Carlos Segura as well as his client.

Design Firm: Segura Inc.
Art Director/Designer: Carlos Segura
Photographer: Geof Kern
Client: John Cleveland

2 These festive "ornaments" make a memorable statement in this holiday mailer for a construction firm. Richardson or Richardson received many appreciative letters from recipients of the promotion who were delighted by its wit.

Design Firm: Richardson or Richardson
Art Director: Rosemary Connelly
Designer: Forrest Richardson
Copywriters: Rosemary Connelly, Forrest Richardson
Client: Rowland Construction

3 (Opposite) This holiday self-promotional mailing catches the attention of its recipients and states the philanthropic mission of its sender. "Instead of giving $2,000 to the local wine shop for traditional Christmas gifts, a donation on behalf of our clients went to help kids with cancer at the 'Hole in the Wall Gang' camp," says firm principal Frank Oswald.

Design Firm: WYD Design, Inc.
Art Director: Frank J. Oswald
Designer: Scott Kuykendall
Copywriter: Frank J. Oswald

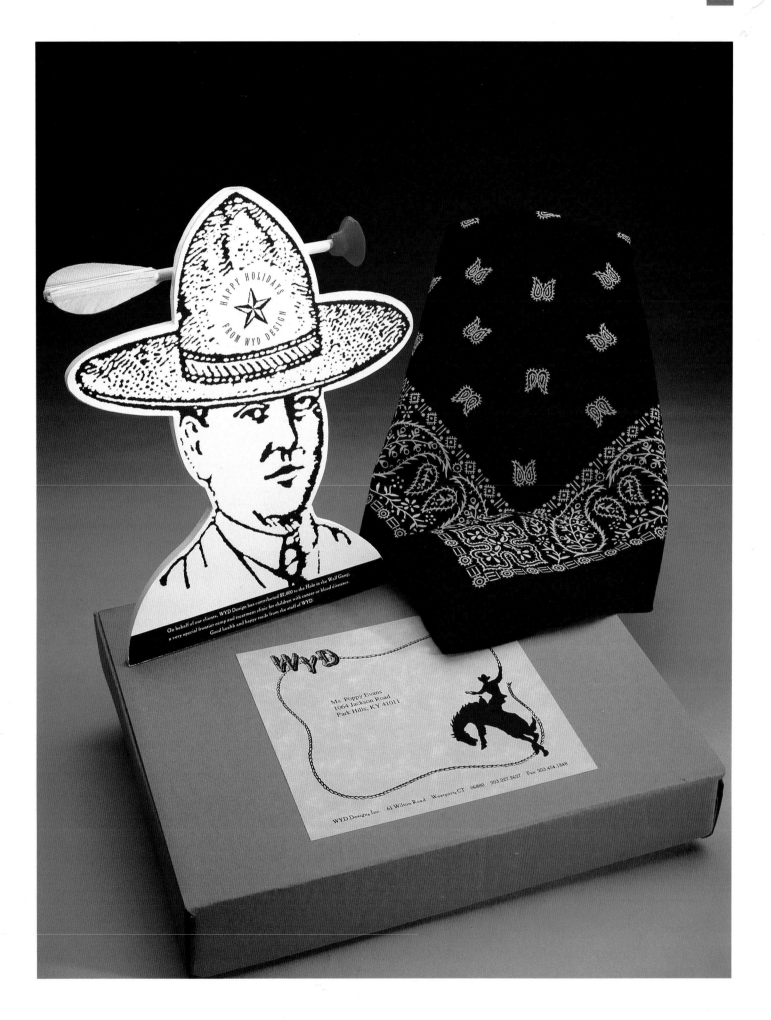

1

2

1 According to illustrator Adam Cohen, the unusual format of this illustrated cube, mailed in a simple white box, never fails to catch the attention of prospective clients. "I've received letters and phone calls from people who have seen it and want one," says Cohen.

Design Firm: Adam Cohen Illustrator
Art Director/Designer/Illustrator: Adam Cohen
Client: Adam Cohen Illustrator

2 This card and gift of a custom-designed sweatshirt went out to clients and vendors over the holidays. As wearable art, the sweatshirt helped to increase visibility for Shimokochi Reeves. "We do this as our holiday promotion every year," says firm principal Anne Reeves. "People love them."

Design Firm: Shimokochi/Reeves
Art Director/Designer: Mamoru Shimokochi, Anne Reeves
Client: Shimokochi/Reeves

1

2

1 It's hard to ignore or forget this exhuberant assortment of goodies, hand-assembled in a custom package and sent to potential and existing clients as a holiday greeting.

Design Firm: Modern Dog
Art Director/Designer: Robynne Raye, Michael Strassburger
Illustrator: Michael Strassburger

2 "Pentagram Papers" is a series of promotional brochures that the design firm sends on a regular basis to prospective and existing clients. This particular mailer, focusing on skeletons, was sent around Halloween.

Design Firm: Pentagram
Art Directors: John McConnell, Woody Pirtlc
Designer: Woody Pirtle
Photographer: Bill Whitehurst
Illustrator: Steven Guarnacia
Client: Pentagram

1 This unique self-promotion, packaged in an authentic fur box, helped to land some big-time clients such as Fox Television and Capitol Records.

Design Firm: Modern Dog
Art Director: Michael Strassburger
Designers: Michael Strassburger, Robynne Rayet, V. Costarella
Client: Modern Dog

2 Bringing ideas to life through illustrations of idioms is the theme of this brochure. Firm principal Scott Hull says it was conceived to have staying power. "I thought it would serve as a source that our clients could refer to time and again—a piece that would stay on their shelves for years."

Design Firm: Scott Hull Associates, Rickabaugh Graphics
Art Director/Designer: Eric Rickabaugh
Illustrator: Scott Hull Associates
Copywriter: Jeff Morris
Clients: Scott Hull Associates, Rickabaugh Graphics, Emerson Press

The strength of Boelts Bros. Design
lies in unity, among our staff
and with our clients. Our projects
and our baking are inspired by
informed research, strategic planning
and a keen aesthetic sense. The result
is a visually articulate statement,
unparalleled for clear
and creative communication.

Boelts Bros. Design. For those
seeking a compelling, enduring identity
in their marketplace.

BOELTS BROS. DESIGN INC.
14 EAST SECOND STREET, TUCSON, ARIZONA 85705-7752 602-792-1026

1 "We have our mother baking for you," claims Boelts Bros. Design in this self-promotional package of pecan rolls. The firm sends the rolls to new and prospective clients. "When we really want someone's business, we send some of our mom's great cooking," says firm principal Jackson Boelts.

Design Firm: Boelts Bros. Design, Inc.
Art Directors: Jackson Boelts, Eric Boelts
Designers: Jackson Boelts, Eric Boelts, Kerry Stratford
Client: Boelts Bros. Design, Inc.

1 Serving a dual purpose as a gift and example of great packaging design, Vaughn Wedeen's custom-packaged jelly, salsa, and chips goes out to clients over the holidays as a thank-you gift for their business.

Design Firm: Vaughn Wedeen Creative
Art Director: Daniel Michael Flynn, Steve Wedeen, Rick Vaughn
Designer: Daniel Michael Flynn
Illustrator: Bill Gerhold
Client: Vaughn Wedeen Creative

2 "Get a Grip," featuring the work of illustrator Greg Dearth, has brought considerable recogntion to Dearth and Scott Hull & Associates, which represents him. "The brochure has received an award in practically every design competition we've entered it in," notes Hull.

Design Firm: Scott Hull & Associates
Designers: Steve Gabor, Marciak Gabor
Illustrator: Greg Dearth
Clients: Greg Dearth, Beckett Paper

1

2

3

1 "Boelts Bros. design icons were adapted for use on t-shirts as a holiday gift," says firm principal Jackson Boelts. "People loved them so much they called to see if they could buy another one." The shirts arrive wrapped in tissue and placed in a box covered with colorful stickers of Boelts Bros. icon designs.

Design Firm: Boelts Bros. Design, Inc.
Art Directors: Jackson Boelts, Eric Boelts
Designers: Jackson Boelts, Kerry Stratford
Client: Boelts Bros. Design, Inc.

2 "Years of Sweet Success" is the theme of this greeting and gift package mailed between Christmas and New Year's Day. "I received many thank-you calls from clients," says Jackson. The piece also resulted in additional business for designer Angela Jackson from clients and vendors wanting her to produce a similar promotion for their firm.

Design Firm: Angela Jackson Design
Art Director/Designer/Calligrapher: Angela Jackson
Client: Angela Jackson

3 This eye-catching mailing kit is sent to potential clients. It includes a tray of 35mm slides, a notebook of 8-by-10-inch photos, and background information on Sayles Graphic Design.

Design Firm: Sayles Graphic Design
Art Director: John Sayles
Designer: John Sayles
Illustrator: John Sayles
Client: Sayles Graphic Design

1

2

1 Over the years, Dunlavey Studio has created a number of humorous holiday promotional mailings that include a legend and a "keepsake" from the firm's fictitious founder, Cormac Dunleavy. One year the gift was this cookbook.

Design Firm: The Dunlavey Studio, Inc.
Art Director: Michael Dunlavey
Designer: Lindy Dunlavey
Client: The Dunlavey Studio, Inc.

2 Another holiday mailing included "snow balls" from one of Cormac Dunleavy enterprises. According to the enclosed legend, creating permanent snowballs was one way Dunleavy made his fortune in Alaska. After reading the enclosed card stating "Have a Yummy Christmas," some clients actually ate the snowballs.

Design Firm: The Dunlavey Studio, Inc.
Art Director: Michael Dunlavey
Designer: Lindy Dunlavey
Client: The Dunlavey Studio, Inc.

1 This photographer's promotional campaign consisted of five postcards, mailed every three days for two weeks, followed by the mailing of a bound self-mailer which incorporated images from the previously mailed postcards.

Design Firm: Bob Design
Designer: Greg Hom, Matthew Clark
Photographer: Larry Dyer
Client: Larry Dyer Photography

PUTTING ON
THE DOG
♣

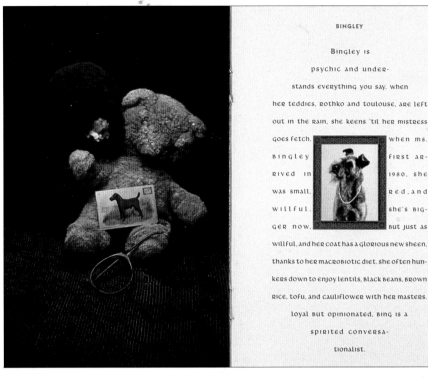

BINGLEY

Bingley is

psychic and under-

stands everything you say. when

her teddies, rothko and toulouse, are left

out in the rain, she keens 'til her mistress

goes fetch. when ms.

bingley first ar-

rived in 1980, she

was small, red, and

willful, she's big-

ger now, but just as

willful, and her coat has a glorious new sheen.

thanks to her macrobiotic diet, she often hun-

kers down to enjoy lentils, black beans, brown

rice, tofu, and cauliflower with her masters.

loyal but opinionated, bing is a

spirited conversa-

tionalist.

WOOF, WOOF.

Bitch, bitch, bitch? never. the irish terrier is a

cheerful and enthusiastic sort of doggy and

an exceptionally game companion, abrim with

daredevil pluck. the tail wags the (toast-

colored) terrier from dawn to dusk. she

keeps burglars at bay and trees raccoons

with equal elan, then cozies up for ear-

scratching at your invitation. beguiling, she's

equally at home in posh parlors and soggy

duck blinds – and is equal to any challenge you

pose, be it fence-jumping or fetch, bird-dog-

ging or babysitting, rat patrol or frisbee. is

she yippy? just enough to intimidate neer-do-

wells. not enough to drive you mad. yippee!

WHAT LOOKS LIKE TOAST BUT JUMPS A
LOT HIGHER?

♣

I

I A tribute to the Irish Terrier provided a great
opportunity for showcasing great photography
and design in this promotional brochure.
"Because the subject matter is not what you
might expect from a design firm, people are
taken off guard and react with a smile," says
firm principal Leslee Avchen.

Design Firm: Avchen and Associates
Art Director: Leslee Avchen
Designer: Leslee Avchen, Garin Ipsen
Photographer: Rick Bell, Terry Heffernan, Judy
Olauson
Client: Avchen and Associates

1

2

1 This series of self-promotional postcards to prospective clients paved the way for follow-up phone calls to arrange portfolio showings.

Design Firm: Mires Design, Inc.
Art Director/Designer: Scott Mires
Designer: Scott Mires
Photographer: Chris Wimpey
Client: Mires Design, Inc.

2 This handmade book was created to promote Studio MD's innovative design style. "By using unconventional materials, it demonstrates our commitment to investigating all avenues for productive results," says art director Jesse Doquilo.

Design Firm: Studio MD
Art Director: Jesse Doquilo, Glenn Mibyi, Randy Lim
Designer: Jesse Doquilo
Client: Studio MD

1

2

1 An environmental theme provided a means of unifying the diverse styles of the many illustrators represented in this colorful brochure.

Design Firm: Mires Design, Inc.
Art Director/Designer: Scott Mires
Client: Celeste Cuomo

2 This client gift of an appointment book and series of calendars was beautifully boxed in a color-coordinated slipcase. It won several awards for its artful design and printing.

Design Firm: Buchanan Printing
Art Director: Lyn Johnson
Designer: David Strand
Illustrator: David Strand
Client: Buchanan Printing

3 (Opposite page) Overprints of CD package designs provided the inserts for this relatively inexpensive promotional mailer. This "Music Box" is sent to recording artists and recording industry executives.

Design Firm: Margo Chase Design
Art Director/Designer: Margo Chase
Photographer: Nels Israelson
Client: Margo Chase Design

SPECIALTY

1 This multicomponent mailer, promoting a national youth convention, arrived in a colorful box that opens to reveal a die-cut brochure and collection of postcards.

Design Firm: Sayles Graphic Design
Art Director/Designer: John Sayles
Illustrator: John Sayles
Client: Open Bible Churches

2 Designed to promote a sales incentive trip, this screw-post bound brochure was mailed in a custom-designed box.

Design Firm: Sayles Graphic Design
Art Director/Designer: John Sayles
Illustrator: John Sayles
Client: National Travelers Life

1

1 A series of swim meets sponsored by Dupont requires a coordinated package of various promotional materials that are mailed to national as well as local media.

Design Firm: Mike Quon Design Offfice
Art Director: Mike Quon, L. Stevens
Illustrator: Mike Quon
Client: Dupont

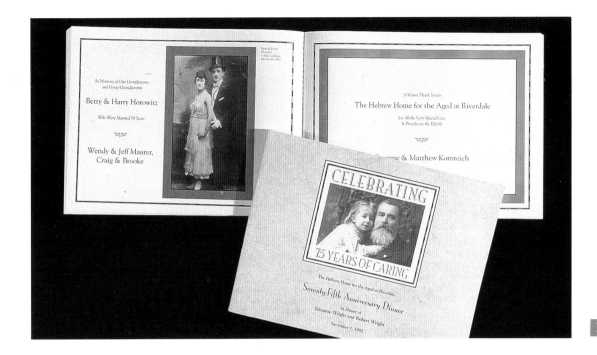

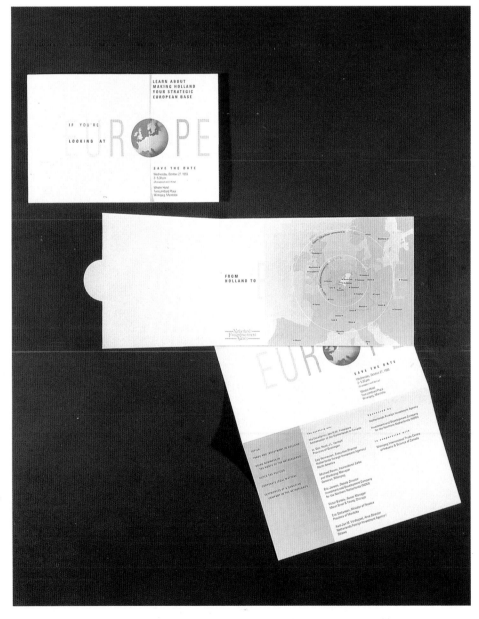

1 As a special fundraising journal, this brochure celebrates the 75th anniversary of a home for the aged. According to its designer, Susan Chait, it raised more than $1 million for the home.

Design Firm: Lebowitz/Gould/Design, Inc.
Art Director: Susan Chait, Sue Gould
Designer: Susan Chait
Client: Molino & Associates, Inc./ The Hebrew Home for the Aged at Riverdale

2 This self-mailer, employing the globe in a circular slot closure, attracted many members of the international business community to the event it promotes.

Design Firm: O&J Design, Inc.
Art Director/Designer: Andrzej J. Olejniczak
Illustrator: Andrzej J. Olejniczak
Client: Ogilvy Adams & Rinehart

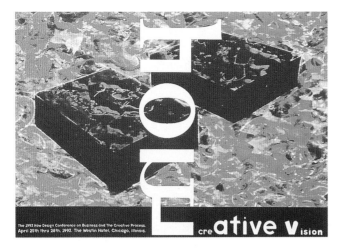

The 1993 How Design Conference on Business and The Creative Process.

April 25th thru 28th, 1993. The Westin Hotel, Chicago, Illinois.

1

1 Creating a promotional campaign for a demanding, design-savvy audience, such as *HOW* magazine's readership, can be a formidable task. This series of postcards promoting *HOW*'s Design Conference stimulated a conference discussion on its unusual graphics (used on other conference materials as well). The postcards also achieved results. "That conference was their most successful one to date," says Segura.

Design Firm: Segura Inc.
Art Director/Designer: Carlos Segura
Client: HOW

1 If you're promoting an event at a restaurant, why not print the information on a napkin? Mailed in a coordinated box, the promotion drew many youngsters who were impressed with its novel approach.

Design Firm: Sayles Graphic Design
Art Director/Designer: John Sayles
Illustrator: John Sayles
Client: Boys & Girls Club of Central Iowa

2 Holiday events at a shopping center are promoted in this eye-catching, tri-panel brochure.

Design Firm: Tracy Sabin, Illustration & Design
Art Director: Marilee Bankert
Designer: Tracy Sabin
Illustrator: Tracy Sabin
Client: Fashion Valley

1

1 This promotional mailing for the Chicago Gift and Accessories Market (a show that brings retailers and wholesalers of gift items together) combines subtle embossing and avocado green to achieve a springlike feeling. According to its designer, Carlos Segura, it drew a record-breaking number of registrants.

Design Firm: Segura Inc.
Art Director/Designer: Carlos Segura
Illustrator: Carols Segura
Client: The Merchandise Mart

2 This poster launched Jones Intercable's "Smart Choice" campaign. It was mailed with a manager's kit to members of the company's sales force.

Design Firm: Vaughn Wedeen Creative
Art Director: Daniel Michael Flynn, Steve Wedeen
Designer: Daniel Michael Flynn
Illustrator: Bill Gerhold
Client: Jones Intercable

2

1

2

1 Promoting a professional meeting at a cartoon theme park required artfully integrating visual elements that represented both. According to designer Mark Oldach, this piece attracted more attendees than the conference could accommodate.

Design Firm: Mark Oldach Design
Art Director/Designer: Mark Oldach
Illustrator: Mark Oldach
Client: American Organization of Nurse Executives

2 This brochure with a futuristic theme drew members of U.S. West's sales force to an annual meeting. Its corrugated surface enabled Vaughn Wedeen to attach an assortment of items to its pages, prompting recipients to browse through the brochure to discover the surprises within.

Design Firm: Vaughn Wedeen Creative
Art Director/Designer: Rick Vaughn
Illustrator: Kevin Tolman, Chip Wyler, Rick Vaughn
Client: U.S. West Communications

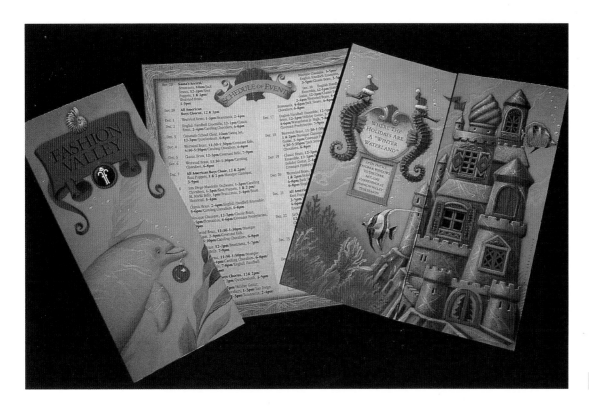

I Holiday happenings at a shopping center were promoted with promotional flyers carrying colorful illustrations. The first mailer was so successful in attracting attention, the client commissioned a similar piece the following year.

Design Firm: Tracy Sabin, Illustration & Design
Art Director: Marilee Bankert
Designer: Tracy Sagin
Illustrator: Tracy Sabin
Client: Fashion Valley

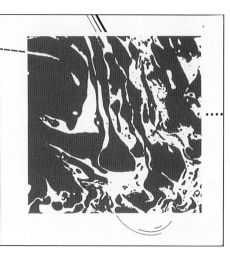

We propose a dialogue about the nature of art, across the boundaries of customary divisions: cross-disciplinary, cross-cultural, cross-historical. Our tendency sometimes seems rooted in defense of territory, a narrowing of focus. We encourage an openness, a stance of participation, a forum for conflict. What are the larger concerns that might unite us rather than separate us?

THE MAP

1

We propose a dialogue about the nature of art, across the boundaries of customary divisions: cross-disciplinary, cross-cultural, cross-historical. Our tendency sometimes seems rooted in defense of territory, a narrowing of focus. We encourage an openness, a stance of participation, a forum for conflict. What are the larger concerns that might unite us rather than separate us?

This conference offers the chance to come together and be stimulated; to re-think what we do; to be renewed, refreshed and enlarged by our experience; and to bring this energy into our work as artists and facilitators of learning–ours as well as that of our students.

THE MAP IS NOT

We propose a dialogue about the nature of art, across the boundaries of customary divisions: cross-disciplinary, cross-cultural, cross-historical. Our tendency sometimes seems rooted in defense of territory, a narrowing of focus. We encourage an openness, a stance of participation, a forum for conflict. What are the larger concerns that might unite us rather than separate us?

This conference offers the chance to come together and be stimulated; to re-think what we do; to be renewed, refreshed and enlarged by our experience; and to bring this energy into our work as artists and facilitators of learning–ours as well as that of our students.

THE MAP IS NOT
THE TERRITORY

We are interested in exploring a more fully engaged range of contact with visual, aural, haptic and kinesthetic experience. We see this not as a new ploy for art but as a way of coming to realize our participation with the world; not our observation of it. Our ideas about the world are not necessarily the world itself. the map is not the territory.

Mid-America College
Art Association
53rd Annual Conference

"The Map Is Not
The Territory"

Omni Netherland Plaza
November 1, 2, 3, 4, 1989
Cincinnati, Ohio

Hosted by the
University of Cincinnati,
College of Design,
Architecture, Art
and Planning

1 This promotional mailer for a seminar on art and society leads the recipient through a series of panels, revealing its message as it unfolds. Designer Stan Brod says that many attended the seminar because of this creative promotion.

Design Firm: Lipson, Alport, Glass & Associates
Art Director: Stan Brod
Designer: Stan Brod
Illustrator: Stan Brod
Client: University of Cincinnati

1 This series of postcards and other promotional items helped to draw a large crowd to Neo-Con '92. "It was really successful for them," says designer Carlos Segura. "Their attendance was larger than ever before."

Design Firm: Segura Inc.
Art Director/Designer: Carlos Segura
Photographer: Geof Kern
Client: The Merchandise Mart

1

1 Brightly colored pop-up graphics make this promotional mailer memorable and fun. It was successful in luring members of the client's sales force to the meeting it promoted and was kept by many recipients who enjoyed its entertainment value.

Design Firm: Sayles Graphic Design
Art Director/Designer: John Sayles
Illustrator: John Sayles
Client: Alexander Hamilton Life

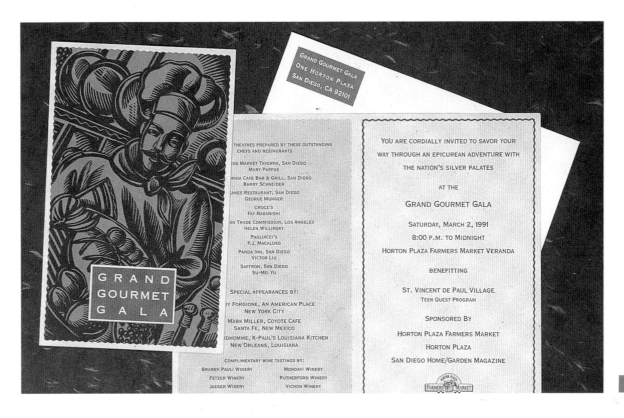

1 This mailer for a local "gourmet gala " plays up renowned chefs and lists their culinary specialties. In addition to drawing a large crowd, the piece won several design awards.

Design Firm: Tracy Sabin, Illustration & Design
Art Director: Linda Natal
Designer: Tracy Sabin
Illlustrator: Tracy Sabin
Client: Horton Plaza Farmer's Market

2 This pre-conference mailing for the ICPA's annual meeting arrived in a burlap bag. Inside is a multi-layered brochure which features branded leather, embossed sheetmetal and silver "conchos" on the cover.

Design Firm: Sayles Graphic Design
Art Director/Designer: John Sayles
Illustrator: John Sayles
Client: Insurance Conference Planners Association

3 Offering a trip as a sales incentive, this packet of goodies went out to U.S. West Communications' sales force. Among the items it includes are play money and a game board.

Design Firm: Vaughn Wedeen Creative
Art Director/Designer: Steve Wedeen
Client: U.S. West Communications

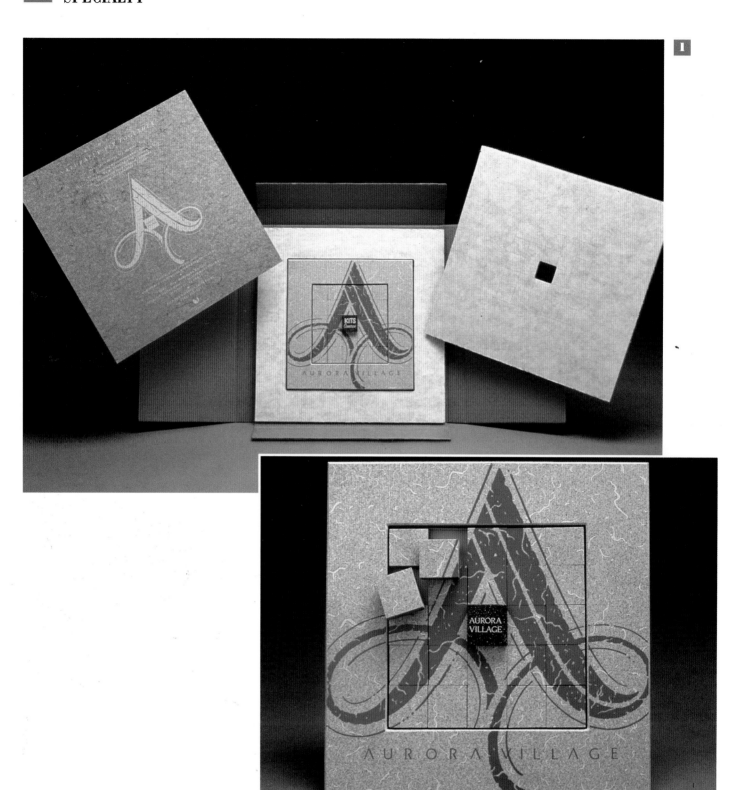

1 This mailer went out to current and prospective tenants to announce a grand opening as well as a new name and graphic identity for a shopping center. Much of its success in attracting attention was due to the interactive aspects of the puzzle it included.

Design Firm: Hornall Anderson Design Works
Art Director: Jack Anderson
Designer: Jack Anderson, Cliff Chung, David Bates
Illustrator: Bruce Hale
Calligrapher: David Bates
Client: Northwest Building Corporation

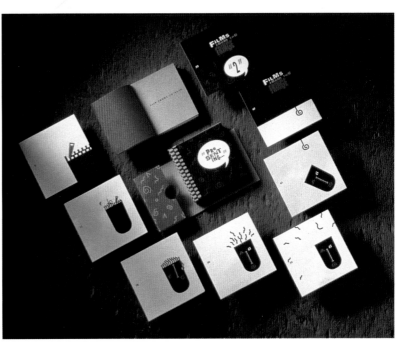

1 An invitation to an award show, sponsored by a local printer, prompted this multicomponent mailer. It included a poster, award certificate, and an invitation which folded into a cube.

Design Firm: Janet Hughes and Associates
Art Director/Designer: Donna Perzel
Photographer: Steve Sharp
Client: Modern Press

2 This invitation to an AIGA event was sent out in the form of a flip book. A pro bono effort, the book was created by a design team of AIGA members and involved donated time from the binder, printer, and many others.

Design Firm: Graphic Communications, Ltd.
Design Team Members: Melanie Bass, Julie Sebastianelli, Richard Hamilton, Andres Tremols, Jim Jackson, Pam Johnson
Illustration: Melanie Bass, Julie Sebastianelli
Copywriter: Jake Pollard
Client: AIGA Washington D.C.

It's a pretty safe bet that if you're going to make it in the creative business, you're going to need to come up with good ideas. And on a regular basis.

To accomplish that, you'll need a place where you can get away from the more mundane aspects of advertising and design... the meetings, the project requisitions, the meetings, the press checks at three in the morning, the meetings, the presentation skills seminars, the meetings, the time sheets, oh, and lest we forget, the meetings.

You need a place where you can think. A place where both sides of your brain can say "Howdy," get to know each other, intermingle, share intellectual high fives, if you will; while you pretty much just keep out of the line of fire and let the creative process happen. Better yet, this place would be able to somehow keep your conscious mind occupied, in order to allow your unconscious mind to put all the pieces together in a new way, to solve the creative problem without distractions or interruptions.

Now, if you were to design such a place, exactly what would it be like? It would probably be white, to suggest openness, freedom of association, limitless possibilities. It would absolutely need to be quiet, so that nothing would disturb your oh-so-delicate thought process. It would hopefully feature walls and fixtures fabricated to be easily wiped clean, so that you could always start fresh, as it were, repeatedly and regularly. Last but not least, to maintain your stream of consciousness, you would insist upon an endless flow of fresh, clean, cool and revitalizing water.

In addition to these basic parameters, of course, your special place will also need something to make it a place you can call your own. Whether it's your back issues of Guns and Ammo, the Best of The Far Side, or just a 2' x 3' throw rug from Pier 1, a little personality goes a long way toward transforming a room from merely functional to purely personal.

There now. You've got the place. You've got the assignments. Now, it's simply a matter of letting it happen. Just remember, when you emerge, flushed with pride, with the killer ideas you developed inside your special place, there's still one more step to take before you can get recognized for all your labors.

You need to enter your work in the 1994 Omni Awards.

Photographer Hollis Officer, and his assistant/model, Eric Bell used a Mamiya RZ camera with Ilford film. He shot the photos at 1/8th and 1/125th of a second. Front and Back Cover

Photographer Dan White, of White & Associates, and his assistants Aaron Bales and Lisa Correu (who also supplied the gams), used a Cannon F-1 camera with a 20 mm lens, and T-MAX film. He used incandescent light in both pictures with different lights inside the bathroom. He also processed the film in a dektol Grand Emporium solution. Musicians' Bathroom

Photographer Nick Vedros and his assistant, Mike McCorkle, had the help of Dale Frommelt to design and build the set for The Dog Bone Lounge. They used a Sinar Bron 4 x 5 camera with T-MAX 100 film, and Comet and Broncolor lighting. The photos were printed on Ilford multigrade paper. Dog Bone Lounge

Photographer David Ludwigs, and his assistant, Kelly Rogers, had the help of stylist, Elaine Hazlett. They used a Mamiya RB67 camera with T-MAX 100 film and a Comet strobe. They used a 37 mm fisheye lens and diffusion printing on the toilet photo. We would like to thank the Kelly Brothers of Kelly's Westport Inn for the use of their bathroom. Kelly's Westport Inn

Photographer Steven Curtis, used a Hasselblad camera with KodakTRI-X film. He shot at 1/125th of a second at F2.8. He also used a special dektol processing technique. Old St. Peter's

Photographer Michael Regnier, used an antique Koropa 11x14 camera (built in 1900) with Super XX film and tungsten lighting. He used the film to make a contact paper negative, and used that to make a contact print on Oriental fiber base paper. Liebstadter Millinery

Photographer Darryl Bertstein, used a Hasselblad camera with T-MAX 100 film and a hand held clamp light. For the photo at the American Royal, he faced death by placing his light in the inside rim of the toilet. Wayne's Harley Grand Emporium Savoy Grill

This call for entry theme was adapted from an original concept created by Muller+Company for Dix & Associates.

Creative: Muller+Company. Paper: Midwestern Paper Company. Printing: Tenth Street Printing Company. Typesetting: Fontastik Inc. Separations: Cicero Graphic Resources Inc, Superior Color Graphics, Chroma-Graphics Inc., Trans America Color Systems.

1 This call for entries for the Kansas City Advertising Club's 1994 Omni Awards features a photo documentary of local restrooms. According to the brochure, these "havens" are places where one can "get away from the more mundane aspects of design...and let the creative process happen."

Design Firm: Muller & Company
Art Director/Designer: John Muller
Photographer: Dan White, Mike Regnier, Hollis Officer, Nick Vedros, Dave Ludwigs, Darryl Bernstein, Steve Curtis
Client: The Advertising Club of Kansas City

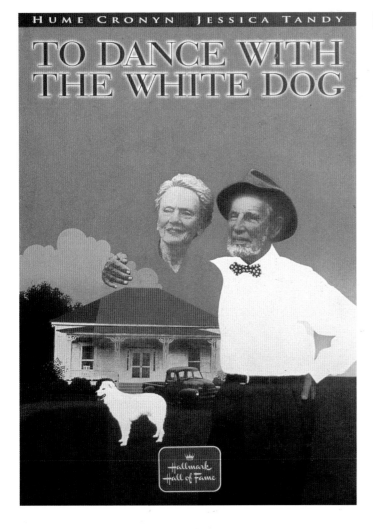

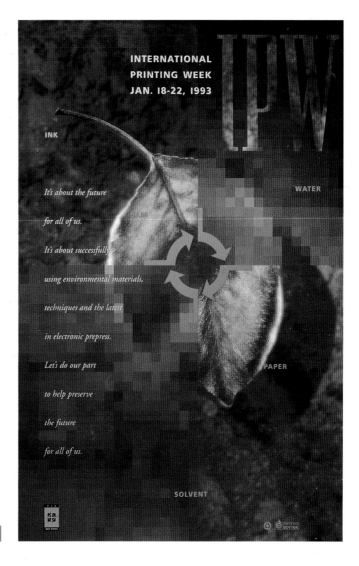

1 Hallmark mailed this folder, filled with a variety of promotional materials, to promote a Hallmark Hall of Fame presentation. The greeting card company also commissioned similar promotional folders from Muller & Company for other Hall of Fame presentations.

Design Firm: Muller & Company
Art Director/Designer: John Muller
Client: Hallmark Card, Inc.

2 The themes of recycling and desktop publishing needed to be stressed in this promotion for a convention of a printer's association. "We chose to portray a leaf and digitize it in an obvious manner," says the promotion's designer Bennett Peji. This image was used on the cover of the convention's promotional brochure as well as on an accompanying poster.

Design Firm: Bennett Peji Design
Art Director/Designer: Bennett Peji
Photographer: John Schulz
Production: Chakra Kusuma
Client: Printing Industries Association of San Diego

1 This brochure was sent to announce a merger between an architectural firm and a design group. Its accompanying business card and stationery helped to establish the firm's new identity in the minds of pre-existing clients.

Design Firm: Hornall Anderson Design Works
Art Director: Jack Anderson
Designer: Jack Anderson, Scott Eggers, Leo Raymundo
Client: Mahlum & Nordfors McKinley Gordon

2 This multicomponent mailer announced the opening of a traveling exhibition and a related fundraising dinner. The sensitive nature of the exhibit's subject matter presented a challenge. "We wanted to evoke an emotional response from the people who received this without going overboard," says its designer David Schultz.

Design Firm: Muller & Company
Art Director/Designer: David Schultz
Client: Kansas City Friends of the N.S. Holocaust Memorial Museum

1

2

1 This attention-grabbing brochure promoted an educational seminar on a new, data management product. It was directed at an audience of upper- and middle-management personnel.

Design Firm: Grafik Communications, Ltd.
Design Team Members: Richard Hamilton, Judy Kirpich
Illustrator: Dynamic Duo
Client: Systems Center, Inc.

2 This unusual poster was printed in two colors on newsprint to promote an annual fundraiser. Forty thousand were printed as a center spread insert for a local newspaper, while 5,000 were reserved for a direct mail campaign.

Design Firm: Puccinelli Design
Art Director: Keith Puccinelli
Designer: Keith Puccinelli, Heidi Palladino
Illustrator: Keith Puccinelli
Client: Santa Barbara Contemporary Arts Forum/Santa Barbara Museum of Art, Friends of Contemporary Art

1 A corporate acquisition marked an occasion for this distinctive mailing announcing the client's acquisition of FORMA from Westin Hotels & Resorts.

Design Firm: Hornall Anderson Design Works
Art Director: John Hornall
Designer: John Hornall, David Bates
Client: FORMA

2 This booklet was used to encourage attendance at an opening event for an exhibit of illustrations by Henrik Drescher at the Library of Congress. "We made Henrik part of our design team," says Grafik design team member Cheryl Clarke. "He had as much to do with the success of this piece as anyone."

Design Firm: Grafik Communications, Ltd.
Design Team Members: Judy F. Kirpich, Jim Jackson, Julie Sebastianelli
Illustrator: Henrik Drescher
Client: Library of Congress

1 This elaborate mailing, which included a plant, poster, and a brochure, was used as a performance incentive. Employees who excelled received it along with a congratulatory letter from Du Pont's vice president.

Design Firm: Janet Hughes and Associates
Creative Director: Donna Perzel
Art Director/Designer: Paul DiCampli
Photographer: John Carter
Client: Du Pont

FREE UNIX® SEMINAR!

Before Time Runs Out

Get Your Multi-vendor UNIX
Network Under Control

1 This series of promotions informed plant managers and executives of the institution of a 24-hour hotline. "The inside contained a sticker with the slogan, 'Du Pont never sleeps,' and their new 800 number," relates firm principal Janet Hughes who helped conceive the promotion.

Design Firm: Janet Hughes and Associates
Art Director/Designer: Donna Perzel
Illustrator: Elwood Smith
Client: Du Pont

2 Pitched to an upper- and middle-management audience, this six-panel, self-mailer promoted an educational seminar that introduced a new data management system.

Design Firm: Grafik Communications, Ltd.
Design Team Members: Jim Jackson, Jennifer Johnson, Lori McKay
Illustrator: Neil Brennan
Client: Systems Center, Inc.

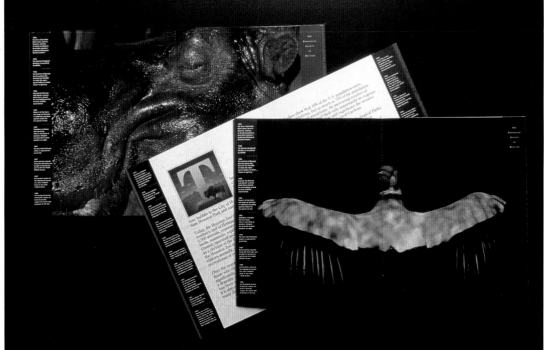

1 This commemorative brochure chronicling the society's history marked the occasion of the Zoological Society of Houston's twenty-fifth anniversary. "We wanted a special edition of their annual report to be a 'coffee table book' that would be kept by the society's supporters." says its designer Lana Rigsby.

Design Firm: Rigsby Design, Inc.
Art Director: Lana Rigsby
Designer: Lana Rigsby, Troy S. Ford
Photographer: Arthur Meyerson
Illustrator: Andy Dearwater
Client: Zoological Society of Houston

1 This invitation to a grand opening of a new facility masqueraded as a CD. The client, an architectural signage firm, was pleased with the large crowd of potential and existing clients it drew.

Design Firm: Al Perez Design
Art Director/Designer: Al Perez
Client: Image Factor

2 An annual partnership-building conference was promoted with this brochure. Its use of simple, two-color iconography, communicates the conference's theme in dramatic fashion.

Design Firm: Hornall Anderson Design Works
Art Director: Jack Anderson
Designer: Jack Anderson, Jani Drewfs, Cliff Chung, Brian O'Neill
Client: Food Services of America

3 (Opposite page) When Du Pont won an environmental achievement award, the company decided to celebrate the occasion with a mailing to its clients. Rather than stress Du Pont's achievement, firm principal Janet Hughes says it was more appropriate to "stress the point that the environment won."

Design Firm: Janet Hughes and Associates
Creative Director: Paul DiCampli
Art Director/Designer: Paul DiCampli
Illustrator: Paul DiCampli
Client: Du Pont

Abrams Design Group 94
Adam Cohen Illustrator 118
Aslan Graphics 67
Avchen and Associates 126
Al Perez Design 154
Angela Jackson Design 123

Bailey Spiker, Inc. 17
Bennett Peji Design 68, 147
Bernhardt Fudyma Design Group 13
Bob Design 125
Boelts Bros. Design, Inc. 8, 11, 32, 41, 109, 111, 115, 121, 123
Brand Design Company 57
The Brownstone Group 42, 52
Buchanan Printing 88, 114, 128
Bukur Design Group 10

Dayton's 11, 19, 22, 23
DBD International 55, 101
Derek Dalton Design 93
Design Horizons International 92
Designsense 107
Dickinson Associates 57
The Dunlavey Studio, Inc. 124

Grafik Communications, Ltd. 43, 48, 50, 56, 78, 145, 149, 150, 152
Graphiculture 113
Gunnar Swanson Design Office 26

Hanson Associates, Inc. 95, 101
Heins Creative, Inc. 114
Herman Miller 31
Hoffman & Angelic Design 16, 102
Holland Mark Martin 34
Hornall Anderson Design Works 36, 58, 60, 62, 100, 144, 148, 150, 154
Hudson's 11, 19, 22, 23

Janet Hughes and Associates I 71, 83, 145, 151, 152, 155
Jane Ross & Associates 12

Kollberg/Johnson Associates 113

Lamson Design 95
Lebowitz/Gould/Design 70, 134
Lewis Design 51
The Levy Restaurants 44
Lipson, Alport, Glass & Associates 140
Little & Company 38, 40, 45, 53, 54, 59
Lowell Williams Design, Inc. 79
Love Packaging Group 8, 88
Lynn St. Pierre Graphic Design 51

Mac By Night Design 16, 66
Marc English: Design 42
Margo Chase Design 129
Mark Oldach Design 21, 24, 138
Marshall Field 11, 19
Metalli Lindberg Adv 6
Mike Quon Design Office 14, 15, 20, 25, 28, 29, 31, 133
Mires Design, Inc 92, 97, 127, 128
Modern Dog 119, 120
Moore Moscowitz 79, 87
Muller & Company 36, 60, 78, 87, 146, 147, 148

Nancy Yerkes Design 58
Nesnadny + Schwartz 81

O&J Design, Inc. 14, 24, 27, 35, 134

Pandamonium Designs 106
Parham Santana, Inc. 25, 85, 102, 111
Pentagram 104, 119
Pictogram Studio 96
Platinum Design, Inc. 34
Puccinelli Design 101, 149

Richardson or Richardson 108, 113, 116
Rickabaugh Graphics 46, 47, 65, 94
Rigsby Design, Inc. 86, 153

Samata Associates 105, 110
Sayles Graphic Design 8, 12, 19, 29, 30, 32, 35, 52, 57, 61, 65, 68, 73, 80, 81, 84, 89, 132, 136, 142, 143
Schmeltz & Warren 39
Scott Hull Associates 120, 122
Segura, Inc. 8, 107, 116, 123, 132, 135, 137, 141
Shimokochi/Reeves 80, 104, 108, 118
Stewart Monderer Design, Inc. 102
Studio MD 127
Supon Design Group 39, 49, 63

Three Fish Design 98, 99
Tieken Design and Creative Services 75
Tracy Sabin Illustration & Design 136, 139, 143
Trickett & Webb Limited 69, 73, 74

Ultimo Inc. 37, 48

Vaughn Wedeen Creative 8, 18, 20, 26, 33, 35, 70, 82, 89, 115, 122, 137, 138, 143

Whitney • Edwards Design 66, 72, 84
WYD Design, Inc. 18, 109, 117

Abrams Design Group
100 View Street
Suite 203
Mountain View, CA 94041
415-964-2388

Adam Cohen Illustrator
96 Greenwich Avenue
New York, NY 10011-7704
212-691-4074

Al Perez Design
713 Patterson Avenue
Glendale, CA 91203
818-243-0940

Angela Jackson
7329 Washburn Way
North Highlands, CA 95660
916-278-7442

Aslan Graphics
6507 Rain Creek Pwy.
Austin, TX 78759
512-346-4742

Avchen and Associates
401 North Third St., #410
Minneapolis, MN 55401
612-339-1206

Bailey Spiker, Inc.
805 E. Germantown Pike
Norristown, PA 19401
215-275-4353

Bennett Peji Design
5145 Rebel Road
San Diego, CA 92117
619-456-8071

Bernhardt Fudyma Design Group
133 E. 36th Street
New York NY 10016
212-889-9337

Bob Design
521 6th Street
San Francisco, CA 94103
415-777-1004

Boelts Bros. Design
14 E. 2nd Street
Tucson, AZ 85705
602-544-4903

Brand Design Company
814 N. Harrison Street
Wilmington, DE 19806
302-888-1648

The Brownstone Group
37 Wellington Avenue
Lexington, MA 02173
617-860-0500

Buchanan Printing
2330 Jett Street
Dallas, TX 75234
214-241-3311

DBD International
38 Park Avenue
Rutherford, NJ 07070
201-896-8476

Derek Dalton Design
174 5th Avenue
New York, NY 10010
212-463-8155

Design Horizons International
520 W. Erie Street
Suite 230
Chicago, IL 60610
312-664-0006

Designsense
P.O. Box 7829
Portland, ME 04112
207-772-4612

Dickinson Associates
37 Wellington Avenue
Lexington, MA 02073
617-860-0500

The Dunlavey Studio, Inc.
3576 McKinley Blvd.
Sacramento, CA 95816
916-451-2170

Grafik Communications, Ltd.
1199 N. Fiarfax St., #700
Alexandria, VA 22314
703-683-4686

Graphiculture
322 First Ave., N., #304
Minneapolis, MN 55401
612-339-8271

Gunnar Swanson Design Office
739 Indiana Avenue
Venice, CA 90291-2728
310-399-5191

Hanson Associates, Inc.
133 Grape Street
Philadelphia, PA 19127
215-487-7051

Heins Creative, Inc.
1242 N. 28th Street
Suite 4A
Billings, MT 59101
406-248-9924

Herman Miller, Inc.
855 E. Main Street
Zeeland, MI 49464-0300
616-654-8248

Hoffmann & Angelic Design
317-1675 Martin Dr.
White Rock, B.C. V4E6E2
604-535-8551

Hornall Anderson Design Works
1008 Western Avenue
Suite 600
Seattle, WA 98104
206-467-5800

Jane Ross & Associates
1685 View Pond, S.E.
Grand Rapids, MI 49508
616-455-2424

Janet Hughes and Associates
3 Mill Road
Wilmington, DE 19806
302-656-5252

Kollberg/Johnson Associaties
7 W. 18th Street
New York, NY 10011
212-366-4320

Lamson Design
652 Main St., 4th Floor
Cincinnati, OH 45202
513-381-6121

Lebowitz/Gould/Design, Inc.
7 W. 22nd St., 7th Floor
New York, NY 10010
212-645-0550

The Levy Restaurants
980 N. Michigan Avenue
Suite 400
Chicago, IL 60611
312-664-8200

Lewis Design
38 Kimball Avenue
Suite 16
Ipswich, MA 01938

Little & Company
1010 S. 7th Street
Minneapolis, MN 55415
612-375-0007 (check)

Lipson, Alport, Glass & Associates.
2401 Ingleside Avenue
Cincinnati, OH 45206
513-861-3368

Love Packaging Group
700 E. 37th St., N.
Wichita, KS 67201
316-832-3369

Lowell Williams Design, Inc.
5650 Kirby Dr.
Suite 260
Houston, TX 77005
713-660-6057

Lynn St. Pierre Graphic Design
3460 Country Village Lane
Trenton, MI 48183
313-692-1248

Mac By Night
22975 Caminito Ouivia
Laguna Hills, CA 92653
714-472-0052

Marc English: Design
37 Wellington Avenue
Lexington, MA 02173
617-860-0500

Margo Chase Design
2255 Bancroft Avenue
Los Angeles, CA 90039
213-668-1055

Mark Oldach Design
3525 N. Oakley Boulevard
Chicago, IL 60618
312-477-6477

Metalli Lindberg Adv.
Via Garibaldi, 5/D
31015 Conegliano
Treviso, Italy
0438-412283

Mike Quon Design Office
568 Broadway
New York, NY 10012
212-226-6024

Mires Design, Inc.
2345 Kettner Boulevard
San Diego, CA 92101
619-234-6631

Modern Dog
601 Valley Street, #309
Seattle, WA 98109
206-282-8857

Moore Moscowitz
99 Chancy Street, #720
Boston, MA 02111
617-482-8180

Muller & Company
4739 Belleview Street
Kansas City, MO 64112
816-531-1992

Nancy Yerkes Design
3715 Duchess, S.E.
Grand Rapids, MI 49506
616-942-2264

Nesnadny + Schwartz
10803 Magnolia Drive
Cleveland, OH 44106
216-791-7721

O&J Design, Inc.
9 W. 29th Street
New York, NY 10001
212-779-9654

Pandamonium Designs
14 Mt. Hood Road
Suite 3
Boston, MA 02135
617-731-8458

Parham Santana
7 W. 18th Street
New York, NY 10011
212-645-7501

Pentagram
212 5th Avenue
New York, NY 10010
212-683-7000

Pictogram Studio
1740 U St., N.W., #2
Washington, DC 20009
202-483-4279

Platinum Design, Inc.
14 W. 23rd Street
New York, NY 10010
212-366-4000

Puccinelli Design
114 E. de la Querra St., #5
Santa Barbara, CA 93101
805-965-5654

Rickabaugh Graphics
384 W. Johnstown Road
Gahanna, OH 43230
614-337-2229

Rigsby Design, Inc.
5650 Kirby Drive
Suite 260
Houston, TX 77005
713-660-6057

Richardson or Richardson
1301 E. Bethany Home Road
Phoenix, AZ 85014
602-266-1301

Samata Associates
101 S. First Street
Dundee, IL 60118
708-428-8600

Sayles Graphic Design
308 Eighth Street
Des Moines, IA 50309
515-243-2922

Schmeltz & Warren
74 Sheffield Road
Columbus, OH 43214
614-262-3055

Scott Hull Associates
68 E. Frankllin Street
Dayton, OH 45459
513-433-8383

Segura, Inc.
361 W. Chestnut
Chicago, IL 60601
312-649-5688

Shimokochi/Reeves
4465 Wilshire Blvd., #100
Los Angeles, CA 90010
213-937-3414

Stewart Monderer Design, Inc.
10 Thacher St., #112
Boston, MA 02113
617-720-5555

Studio MD
1512 Alaskan Way
Seattle, WA 98101
206-682-6221

Supon Design Group, Inc.
100 Connecticut Ave., N.W., #415
Washington, DC 20036
202-822-6540

Three Fish Design
420 N. Fifth Street
Suite 540
Minneapolis, MN 55401
612-375-9444

Tiecken Design & Creative Services
2800 N. Central Avenue
Suite 150
Phoenix, AZ 85004
602-230-0060

Tracy Sabin Illustration & Design
13476 Ridley Road
San Diego, CA 92129
619-484-8712

Trickett & Webb Limited
The Factory
84 Marchmont Street
London WCIN 1AG
071-288-5832

Vaughn Wedeen Creative
407 Rio Grande, N.W.
Albuquerque, NM 87104
505-243-4000

Whitney • Edwards Design
3 N. Harrison Street
Easton, MD 21601
410-822-8335

WYD Design, Inc.
61 Wilton Road
Westport, CT 06880
203-227-2627

ART INSTITUTE OF ATLANTA
LIBRARY